The Price of Honor

Are we who we say we are?

written by
Ozzie Knezovich

ISBN: 978-0-578-71608-4 (Paperback)

Library of Congress Control Number: 2020911693

Some references to historical events and real people have been changed slightly to avoid revealing the identity of parties involved in illegal activities.

Front cover and book design by Dana and Rusty Lynd.

Printed by KDP.

Second printing edition 2022.

Endorsements

"What Ozzie has done with this book, is attempt to capture the true essence of the types of conflict that arises in executive leadership. The need to support your officers and community always, while staying vigilant for how the small things (and sometimes big things) can derail that hard earned public trust. Union protections that our legislators have put in place for all the right reasons for our officers and deputies can easily become abused by a system that is not balanced to ensure that those sworn to uphold the law are themselves held accountable. This is now pulled into the "anti-police" or "pro-police" rhetoric of the election cycles rather than objectively worked as a problem which has viable solutions. Ozzie has done everyone a great service, by boldly pointing out the issues, now we must all get on board with fixing the problem!"

– David Boggs

"As a retired federal agent and corporate executive I have known Ozzie for the majority of time covered by this book. I'm amazed at how he has weathered these storms and never lost his focus, integrity, or dedication. He has truly been Sisyphus, of Greek mythology, constantly rolling a rock uphill."

– Charles Robb

"Sheriff Ozzie Knezovich has stood on the principles of integrity and is not afraid of speaking the truth. In this book, he is setting the record straight. We need more truth speakers as Chiefs and Sheriffs in this country. It takes courage to stand on truth and Sheriff Knezovich has that courage."

– Anne Kirkpatrich

"Extraordinary insights to contemporary challenges in the world of law enforcement leadership. Ozzie provides remarkably candid examples experienced over 4 terms as Spokane County Sheriff, pulls no punches, and provides values-based solutions which have kept him at the top of the list of trusted elected public servants in our community. A must read for anyone interested in the politics of law enforcement!"

– Neal Sealock
Brig Gen US
Army Retired

Acknowledgements

Thank God for grandmothers who teach God first, followed by family, love of country, hard work, service, and kindness to others - especially the downtrodden. I am thankful for my grandmother Mary's constant reminder that, "The only thing you truly own is your name. Do nothing to dishonor it, boy."

To my wife, Paula, who has followed me around the world, seen many things with me, struggled through hard times next to me, and braced me up when the weight of the world seemed a little much. You are the strength of the machine.

To my father who said, "If you're going to do it, do it right."

To all the coaches, teachers, and extended family members who kept a lone wolf kid on the right path.

To the Spokane community, thank you for the support and friendship you have given me over these many years.

And most importantly, to my God and my Savior, who is my rock and my salvation.

Dedication

This book is dedicated the men and women of law enforcement who go to work each shift and perform your duties with honor, humility, and a sense of service to the communities you love. All too often society forgets the great challenge it has placed upon your shoulders and can be all too quick to judge how you perform one of the most challenging jobs there is.

The book is also dedicated to your families. The ones who worry about you every day and who watch silently as you struggle to deal with the horrors you see and do your best to keep hidden. They, too, walk and ride the beat with you and share in your struggles to make sense of a society that has forgotten that you are the good guys.

To my Brothers and Sisters, you will never be forgotten.

Sheriff Ozzie's Thoughts on Leadership and Relationships

"Things would be a lot better if people could simply drop their emotional luggage and move on without it."

"Rare is the day that buy-in = 100%."

"Don't mistake buy-in for like-in."

"Controlling one's behaviors and maintaining relationships are the key to leadership survival."

"The troops always suffer when leadership is at war with itself."

"People follow what they trust, people trust what they know. To be followed, you need to be trusted, to be trusted you need to be known."

"I know that I am not the same person I was 14 years ago nor 33 years ago. I made mistakes; I still make mistakes. It is what you learn from and do with those mistakes that determine the type of leader you become. Those who learn and fix their shortcomings become great leaders."

Emotions and personal agendas are poison to not only relationships and partnerships but to one's own leadership abilities.

"The Chain of Command". To me, "Chain" is a fitting term for it.

"Leading is not about keeping/making friends, it's about taking care of people, treating everyone fairly, and sometimes making difficult decisions that not everyone will understand or agree with.

Table of Contents

Organization Chart

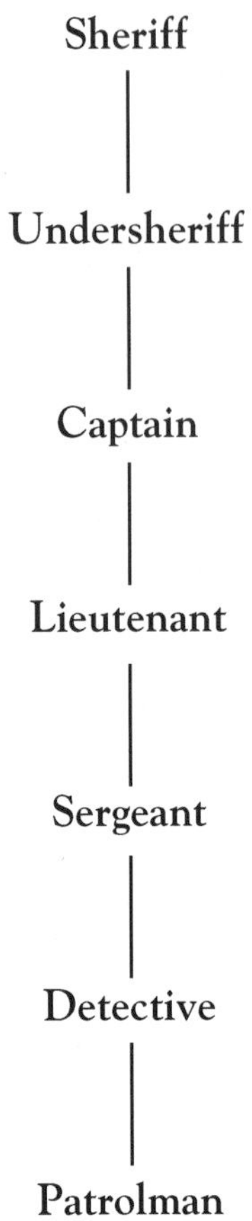

Introduction

Before and during my 2018 election cycle, I was asked many times by those closest to me, "Sheriff, why run again?" They knew the challenges I had faced in my profession over the years, especially between 2013 and 2018. Many said "I wouldn't take your job if they paid me a million dollars a year. The purest answer was, and still is, I believe in you, the American people. I want to help you make our communities great places to live, raise a family, and work. I do what I do because I still believe in this country. I believe that we, as a people, can and must find a way to truly live up to the American dream—the idea that all people are created equal and that there is liberty and justice for all.

Tragically on the eve of publishing this book, an event occurred which once again placed my profession under the white-hot spotlight of the world's attention. On May 25, 2020, George Floyd died at the hands of a Minneapolis police officer, Derek Chauvin. Within days of his death, many began protesting the killing of Mr. Floyd. Sadly, the righteous outcry concerning this inexcusable death was highjacked by riots promoted by others with their own agendas. Agendas that had nothing to do with the pain felt by the African American community.

Something else happened as a result of this senseless, unjustifiable death. Something I have attempted to drive into the hearts of the deputies who work for the Spokane County Sheriff's Office and police officers I meet. When one of us does something bad, we all wear it. Every one of our badges became tarnished by that event. Mr. Floyd's death at the hands of a rogue police officer once again splashed shame on the badges of all of us who serve our communities.

Is it fair? Is it right? No. Because 99% of us who choose to serve, do it right. We live up to the Oaths we took to protect and serve. Such is the price for wearing a badge. Our badges represent the highest ideas, values, and standards of a society. Our badges represent honor, character, courage, and all the other words we hang on the walls of our respective agencies. We took an Oath to live our lives by a higher standard than anyone in society. We took the Oath to represent the very best in humanity, to serve humanity, to protect humanity, and to give our lives if necessary, to save yours. The death of George Floyd represents none of these qualities. We must demand more of ourselves; we must live up to the values we profess to have.

Now, once again, we see fear, anger, and hate rising in our communities. Sadly, if the activists, politicians, and media stoking these emotions would stop long enough to listen, the echo they would hear is America's nearly one million police officers, sheriff deputies, federal agents, chiefs, and sheriffs saying, "You are right. What happened to George Floyd should not have happened and must never happen to anyone ever again."

Fear, anger, hate. Emotions easily highjacked by people with agendas and turned into radicalized hate. Radicalized hate kills. And no side of the political spectrum is immune.

On July 7, 2016, I watched an insidious kind of hate kill five Dallas police officers. Those Dallas police officers died protecting people who had come to protest against them, to call them murderers and racists. Those police officers died because leadership at every level of this country failed them and our nation. I see the same thing happening today. I see leadership failing once again. I fear this day will continue to repeat itself if we don't find a way to come together and solve the many issues that have caused so much death on both sides.

We, the law enforcement and political leaders at all levels, saw that night in Dallas coming. Leadership was complicit in, even aided, the events that took place. We let those Dallas police officers, their families, their friends, their agency, and their community down. We allowed a false narrative to be driven at a high-pitch volume. We allowed those Dallas officers to be killed by an old hate that had been made new by lies told by activists and false news reports. We allowed our nation to hear that their police officers were evil and were ready to kill them without provocation. We allowed the false narrative to continue. A narrative that claimed that our police officers use unjustified force as a routine practice. We, the leadership from the highest seat down, allowed race to be weaponized in order to inflame the message of hate toward all police officers.

I changed that day. I realized that the only way to stop this evil was to confront it and its messengers head on.

For me, July 7, 2016, will forever be the day America's leadership failures could no longer go unchallenged. I would not simply raise a passive warning while our nation was pulled apart by radicalized hate from both the left and the right. I could no longer watch our leaders bend to the loudest voices instead of leading us with conviction and courage toward a more perfect union. It was time to do something to combat this radicalized hate. So, I began writing this book because I know that words are more powerful than anything else.

I love my county, and I refuse to let this evil pull it apart. I have watched those who embrace radicalized hate and its tactics of intimidation force good people out of elected office. They have nearly erased fifty years of progress in terms of race relations in our country. They exist on both the left and the right, and they are killing the country so many of us love and believe in.

There are some things worth fighting for, folks.

Truth, honor, character, integrity—these are things we once held in great regard.

As a result of George Floyd's death, activists, politicians, Hollywood,

athletes, and media talking heads are once again demanding police reform. The same tired old cry of, "The police need more training!" New legislation is being crafted at lightning speed in Congress to "fix the police." As if a bunch of rushed half measures made by Congress has ever helped any situation. They have little to no understanding about the true issues behind this problem.

Mom and Pop America, you are being lied to. Those police officers in Minneapolis knew what they were supposed to do. Listen to the video. You can hear them say, "Roll him on his side." It wasn't lack of training. It was lack of values, standards, and courage to do the right thing. Courage to knock Chauvin off Floyd's neck and roll him on his side. Training that is not built on the solid foundation of values and standards means nothing.

Some ask why police officers with negative employment histories get to keep their jobs. Because police chiefs and sheriffs lack the strong tools required to get rid of bad police officers.

This book is about the struggle of law enforcement leaders to change a system that makes it nearly impossible to remove bad police officers from our ranks. It shows how all thirty-nine Sheriffs of the State of Washington went to these same politicians who are now screaming for reform, and asked them to change state law in order to make it impossible for an arbitrator to give a bad police officer their job back if we proved that they had lied or committed a crime on duty. These same politicians said, "NO!" We couldn't even get the bill out of committee.

These so-called political leaders sold out to the largest campaign donations. My peers and I were told, "Have you lost your minds? Have you forgotten who runs the State of Washington? The unions."

The heart of our nation is failing because our leaders no longer lead. Instead, they appease and condone bad behavior, all for a higher vote count or for fear they may alienate part of their base. Sadly, few leaders still possess the character or courage necessary to truly lead.

It takes courage to stand one's ground when you're faced with the dark reality of your own professional demise. I faced that dark reality when I was told, "Sheriff, if you don't back down now, we're coming after you."

I survived.

Leaders quickly learn one overarching truth: true leadership comes at a cost. It means some folks will not like you. People who don't share your values will be more than willing to destroy you, should you have the audacity to stand your ground for what is right. The folks who came after me, and who continue to do so, don't like me because I stand against the hate they preach and because I stand for values that they only give lip service to. These are people who do not know honor.

The fight is much deeper than I can possibly cover in this book. The forces involved are much larger than just a simple sheriff's race. It is all a piece of a much larger fight that is currently being waged in our towns and states across this great country. It's a fight for the heart of America. I find myself compelled to do something. I couldn't just retire and leave this mess to the next generation. The stakes are too high.

Now, more than at any other time in the history of American law enforcement, we need leaders who are willing to hold the line, join hands with the citizens we protect, and reunite our communities and, ultimately, our nation. Mom and Pop America still believes in its law enforcement. The real question is: Does America's law enforcement still believe in itself?

More importantly, are we willing to hold ourselves to the higher standards we claim to live by? We must uphold these standards in all we do if we are to be worthy of that most sacred honor bestowed upon us by those we protect.

What is that honor? It is their trust in us.

We are the physical symbols of liberty and justice—liberty to lead lives free from fear, and justice for those harmed by crime.

The public's trust is our strongest bond with the people we took an oath to protect. We must always serve in such a way that this trust is never lost.

We live in a time when the art of leadership is dying, a time when people openly lament the possibility that there are no true leaders left. Now, perhaps more than ever, we need leaders who are willing to take a stand for all we once held to be right. We need leaders who are willing to stand for honor.

Honor has a price. It's time to decide if we are willing to pay it.

Chapter 1
Latte & Sausage

"He did what? What do you mean he 'exposed himself' to a barista?"

"Sheriff, according to the police report, our detective apparently knew the barista and was there to sell her some sausage."

"Sausage? Really? You can't make this stuff up."

This was a conversation I had with a member of my command staff within a month of being appointed Sheriff. A detective from our agency had delivered some sausage to the barista at the coffee stand where she worked. Afterward, he drove around to the drive-thru window and, when the barista came to the window, he had his penis in his hand and asked her if she wanted more sausage.

Our conversation continued:

"And he confessed to doing this?"

"Yes."

To make things worse, he was my friend. He had worked for me when I was the agency's training sergeant. He was responsible for writing policy and making sure the agency was ready for re-accreditation. This is a guy I had played racquetball with three times a week for over a year.

The agency was in an uproar, with everyone debating what needed to happen next. For me, the answer was very clear and very simple. At least, that's what I thought. But there were those in the agency who were beating the "it's only a misdemeanor" drum.

I couldn't help thinking, "Let me get this straight. First, one of our detectives exposed himself to a barista in public. Second, while exposing himself, he, in a very unique way, asked her if she wanted to have sex with him. Third, he confessed, which was supposed to make it all better. And fourth, because it was only a misdemeanor and he was being honest, I was expected to look the other way and simply slap his hand for embarrassing the agency as well as every police officer

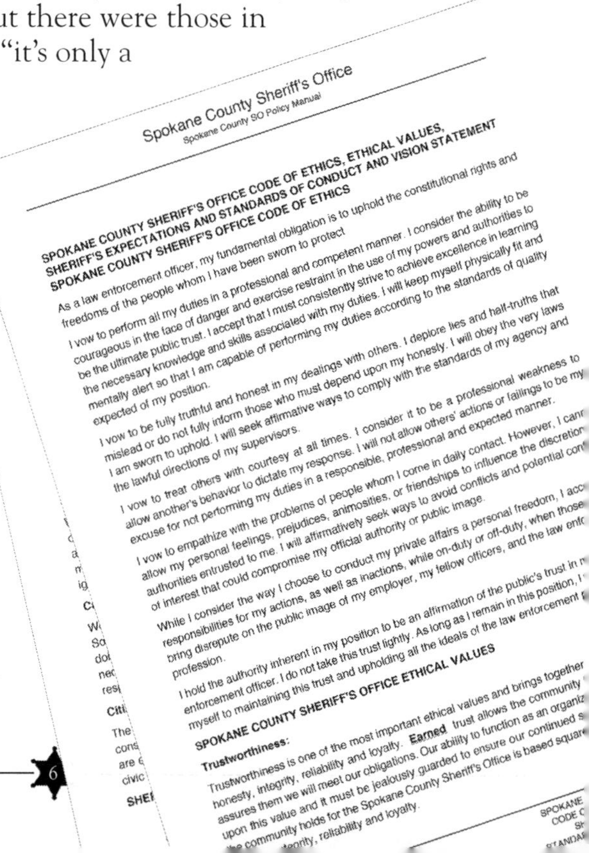

Spokane County Sheriff's Office
Spokane County SO Policy Manual

SPOKANE COUNTY SHERIFF'S OFFICE CODE OF ETHICS, ETHICAL VALUES, SHERIFF'S EXPECTATIONS AND STANDARDS OF CONDUCT AND VISION STATEMENT

SPOKANE COUNTY SHERIFF'S OFFICE CODE OF ETHICS

As a law enforcement officer, my fundamental obligation is to uphold the constitutional rights and freedoms of the people whom I have been sworn to protect

I vow to perform all my duties in a professional and competent manner. I consider the ability to be courageous in the face of danger and exercise restraint in the use of my powers and authorities to be the ultimate public trust. I accept that I must consistently strive to achieve excellence in learning the necessary knowledge and skills associated with my duties. I will keep myself physically fit and mentally alert so that I am capable of performing my duties according to the standards of quality expected of my position.

I vow to be fully truthful and honest in my dealings with others. I deplore lies and half-truths that mislead or do not fully inform those who must depend upon my honesty. I will obey the very laws I am sworn to uphold. I will seek affirmative ways to comply with the standards of my agency and the lawful directions of my supervisors.

I vow to treat others with courtesy at all times. I consider it to be a professional weakness to allow another's behavior to dictate my response. I will not allow others' actions or failings to be my excuse for not performing my duties in a responsible, professional and expected manner.

I vow to empathize with the problems of people whom I come in daily contact. However, I cann allow my personal feelings, prejudices, animosities, or friendships to influence the discretion authorities entrusted to me. I will affirmatively seek ways to avoid conflicts and potential con of interest that could compromise my official authority or public image.

While I consider the way I choose to conduct my private affairs a personal freedom, I acc responsibilities for my actions, as well as inactions, while on-duty or off-duty, when those bring disrepute on the public image of my employer, my fellow officers, and the law enfo profession.

I hold the authority inherent in my position to be an affirmation of the public's trust in m enforcement officer. I do not take this trust lightly. As long as I remain in this position, I myself to maintaining this trust and upholding all the ideals of the law enforcement

SPOKANE COUNTY SHERIFF'S OFFICE ETHICAL VALUES

Trustworthiness:

Trustworthiness is one of the most important ethical values and brings together honesty, integrity, reliability and loyalty. **Earned** trust allows the community assures them we will meet our obligations. Our ability to function as an organiz upon this value and it must be jealously guarded to ensure our continued s community holds for the Spokane County Sheriff's Office is based squar integrity, reliability and loyalty.

and deputy in the area, and for damaging the most valuable thing those of us in law enforcement have, which is the public's trust."

The logic of the above argument made my head hurt. It was clear what had to be done. The detective could no longer be allowed to wear the badge. He had dishonored it and had lost the great privilege the people had given him: the privilege of serving them. They had trusted him to uphold the Oath we all swear when we begin our careers.

The rest of the week was a blur of activity to make sure that the termination process was handled correctly. On the day of his termination hearing, the detective met me as I was walking into the Public Safety Building. I greeted him. He shook my hand, looked me in the eye, and told me that he would lose all respect for me if I didn't do the right thing. He then apologized for putting me in such a position. I thought to myself, "Now, that's the guy I know, taking responsibility for his actions and willing to face the consequences."

We walked into the building, and he waited in the hallway as I met with members of my command staff and my attorney. After a short conference, we met the detective and his union representatives. The detective gave his side of the event, admitted to committing the offence, and apologized.

It was this event that made me swear that I would always hold onto one very hard and fast rule: Never terminate someone unless you are looking them in the eye.

Never terminate someone unless you are looking them in the eye.

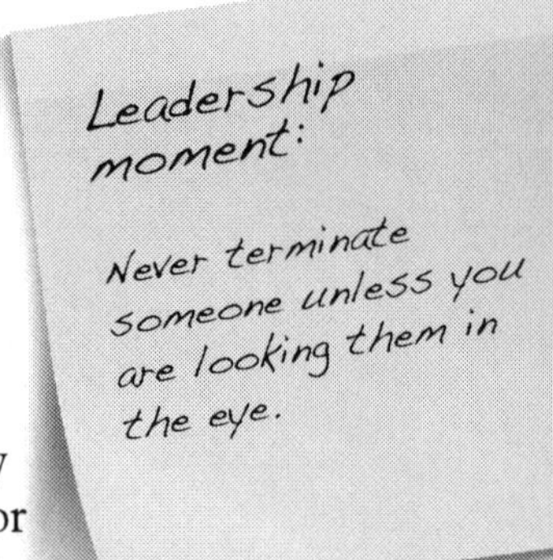

This rule was formed by two principles:

1) The closest thing to killing someone you will ever do is to fire them. You are taking everything they have away from them: the way they feed their family, maintain the roof over their heads, everything.
2) Anyone who says terminating someone is easy has either: Never had to terminate someone, or (perhaps most importantly) they should never be placed in a position where they can do so, because terminating someone should rarely be easy.

Looking someone in the eye as you are about to fire them gives you a chance to have a final gut check to make sure that you have done your job right. It allows you to search your mind to ensure that you know all the information about the case, that you have carefully weighed the information, that you have checked for any mitigating circumstances to select the appropriate discipline, and that you know in your heart that there is no way to lessen the discipline while still fulfilling your professional responsibilities.

As law enforcement leaders, we must balance the offense against our duty to uphold our Oath, our duty to make sure our employees are treated fairly, and most importantly, our duty to ensure the public's rights are protected. In doing so, we strive to maintain the public's trust.

With all of this in mind, I announced that his employment with the Spokane County Sheriff's Office was terminated, effective immediately.

What happened next?

Little did I realize that the fallout from this event would propel me through my first election in 2006, having just been appointed interim Sheriff a month prior. This termination would change the face and dynamics of the Spokane Civil Service Commission, and it would define my next seventy-five terminations in a span of thirteen years.

The media hit hard and fast. They speculated that this would be my litmus test to see if I would hold deputies accountable or let them slide. I could understand their skepticism. My opponent took every opportunity to point out that I had been the president of our union, the Spokane County Deputy Sheriff's Association (DSA), for five years prior to my appointment. Their favorite line was, "If you want a 'union hack' running the Sheriff's office, then vote for Ozzie."

I had heard all kinds of speculation. How long would it take me to have the event investigated? How long would it take me to make a decision concerning what the discipline would be? What level of discipline would I hand out? It seemed the going wager was that I would delay any decision until after the primary election and that the punishment, if any, would be a slap on the wrist. Because, you know, I was just a union hack.

I shattered this image when, within five days, the event was investigated, the employment hearing was held, and the termination announcement was made. Suddenly, the media was stating that "not only is there a new Sheriff in town," but this one is a "different kind of Sheriff."

This has always amazed me in some respects, but in other respects, not so much. They didn't know me. Even the people within the Sheriff's Office didn't seem to remember that for most of my working life, I was the one people came to when a hard or unpopular decision had to be made. If those within the agency had been watching, they would have known what I would do based on the way I had handled several disciplinary issues as their union president.

On more than one occasion I had to tell one of my union members, "You've really stepped in it, and there is not much that I'm going to do for you. Your best bet is to go in with your hat in your hand, fall on your sword, and hope the old man sees it your way." Why the speech? Because I can't stand lazy or dirty police officers and I don't like working with them.

I grew up in a union family. My great-grandfather, my grandfather, my father, and I were coal miners. Union coal miners. United Mine Workers of America coal miners. In our house, John L. Lewis was almost godlike.

I vividly remember the issues surrounding union rights being discussed around the kitchen table. I stood my first picket line with my dad at the age of eleven. I remember the shame the family felt when one of the family crossed that picket line.

So I was—and to some extent still am—union at my core. I say "to some extent" because I truly feel that unions have lost their heart. They used to stand for safe working conditions first and family wage jobs second. And they did not protect slugs. Everyone was expected to do their job and do it right.

Not so much anymore. The unions of today seem more interested in protecting bad actors than holding them to standards.

This new reality is not the reality I learned around the kitchen table. Woe to the man who was known as a slacker because he wouldn't be around long. A man's worth was measured by how honest he was and how hard he worked. Because of my upbringing, when my son asked me what he should do in life that would make me proud, I told him "I don't care what you do in life or how much money you make. As long as you're known as an honest, hard-working man. What more could I ever ask for?" This is what I learned as a child at my parents' and grandmother's kitchen table. This is what I taught my children at my own kitchen table.

But back to my first termination. It was the union element that first worried me. I heard rumors that the union might fight the detective's termination. I was assured by a friend that the issue swung in my favor simply because the union didn't want to fight this termination in public. I wish I could say that this was because they believed that a cop who exposes himself should be terminated. Nope, they just wanted to avoid the bad press.

Without the union behind him, the detective was left with only one avenue open if he wanted to keep his job. He could appeal the termination to the Civil Service Commission, which he did. This appeal would result in a major public uproar.

Once the Civil Service Commission accepted the case, something happened that was totally contrary to the reason Civil Service Commissions were originally formed: politics came into play.

Definition of Civil Service Commissions:
The Civil Service Commission was instituted in the 1950s to prevent unethical hiring and promotion practices by elected officials. The Civil Service Commission oversees the hiring, promotions, and disciplinary practices of the Sheriff. Members of the Commission are citizen volunteers who are appointed by a County's Board of County Commissioners.

A leader has to be willing to be criticized for doing the right thing.

Leaders need to understand that they have to be comfortable with criti-

cism when they do the right thing. Your detractors will paint whatever you do as self-serving, even if they admit it was the best thing you could have done.

In this case, one of the Civil Service Commissioners, who was also a supporter of my opponent, began stating that the only reason I terminated the detective was so I could win the election. He even stated this position in the hearing.

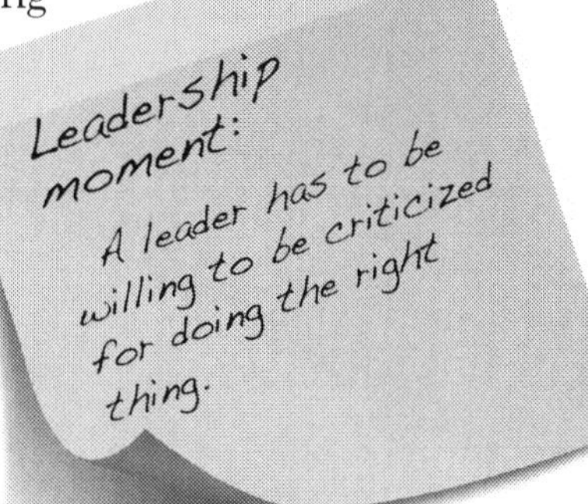

On the night of the Civil Service hearing, there were only two Commissioners present, one who had supported me and one who had supported my opponent in the election. The Commissioner who sided with my opponent attacked me for the supposed "political undertones" of the termination. He then minimized the detective's actions and demanded that the detective be reinstated, which he was.

In response, the other Commissioner demanded that the detective be put on paid leave and forced to retire two months later.

To say the least, I was dumbfounded by the decision. I was told not to worry about it because the detective had ultimately lost his job. What a misguided statement. It didn't seem to matter that the negotiated settlement actually gave the detective his job back before forcing him to retire.

You may be thinking, "So what's the big deal?"

Let me explain. The idea that police officers are not held accountable was reinforced in the public eye when he got his job back, further damaging the public image of law enforcement. This idea was especially used by activists and politicians from 2014 on to justify more controls on police officers. Their drum beat is always: "No one holds police officers accountable," or "the police always get away with everything." When asked by the media for a comment concerning the ruling, all I could say was, "What does it take to get fired?"

The ruling sent shockwaves through the community. Letters to the editor harshly chastised the Civil Service Commission for their decision. There were calls for the County Commissioners to replace the Civil Service Commissioners. Citizens thanked me for taking a hard stand. The case resulted in the resignation of both Commissioners, and ultimately a total restructuring of the Civil Service Commission as a whole.

The termination would be a seminal event for my career as Spokane County Sheriff in many ways. It represented my first termination, which was overturned because of politics, not because it was a wrongful termination. It would be the prelude to two other overturned terminations resulting in my quest to change state law.

It also represented the beginning of my ongoing fight against arbitrators who protect corrupt police officers and deputies, people who should never be allowed to wear a badge. Over the course of the next thirteen years, I would terminate seventy-five additional members of the Spokane County Sheriff's Office, all because they chose to dishonor the badge. Five of those terminations were overturned, not because I did something wrong in the termination process (a common claim by the unions and political opponents), but because arbitrators gave the offending officers their jobs back despite the facts. Each time this happened, it left me to figure out what to do with deputies and correction officers who had proven they cannot be trusted.

The issues I introduce in this book are not new, nor are they unique to the Spokane County Sheriff's Office. I will say, however, that they are the exception and not the norm.

During my time as Sheriff, I studied and compared the disciplinary issues I was facing with those faced by my predecessors. In doing so, I ran across this memo. The lieutenant who wrote it was the best lieutenant I have ever had the pleasure of serving under.

THIRD SHIFT BULLETIN - (TSB #3)"
June 12, 1992

Misconduct, discipline, ethics, professionalism – these have been common topics in the media and in our department lately. Why should the public trust us with the authority to take away an individual's freedom, the authority to forcefully enter private residences and search, or with the authority to use deadly force? Does each of us serve the public or do we or at least some of us prefer to serve ourselves? Do you believe in the mission of the Sheriff department or do you work for a paycheck and nothing more? Some of the recent events involving jailers, deputy sheriffs, and police officers should cause each of use to pause, reflect, and ask ourselves these kinds of questions.

Webster's defines ethics as "the discipline dealing with moral duty and obligation." During the remainder of the mark-up I will be meeting with each of the deputies assigned to Third Shift. We will discuss professional and ethical conduct, values, the role of discipline, and my expectations for the conduct of deputies. If you have questions about any aspects of the recent termination of a Third Shift deputy I will answer them fully at that time.

Mike Aubrey

Today, across the United States, we have law enforcement leaders facing these same issues. They are trying their best to uphold the values of our profession and galvanize those values in those they supervise. Most law enforcement leaders work to ensure the honor of their profession, only to be undermined by a political and legal/arbitration system that seems dedicated to eroding the very foundations of the values we hold to be essential. These values are the cornerstones of all we say we are and are essential to maintaining the public's trust.

In the next chapter, I will introduce two of these arbitration cases, and I will explain why one led all thirty-eight of my fellow sheriffs in the State of Washington to join me in an attempt to pass a bill that simply stated, "Police officers should not commit crimes on duty, nor should they lie."

The bill also stated, "If an arbitrator finds that said officer committed the offence/offences, and if the arbitrator also finds the Sheriff or Chief has followed the termination process and labor laws, the arbitrator cannot change the Sheriff or Chief's disciplinary decision."

Basically, we tried to pass a law that would prevent a law enforcement officer who has lied or who has broken the law on duty from being able to wear a badge.

I learned that there truly is a price for upholding honor, a heavy price that can end your career and ultimately result in your own honor being unjustly tarnished. It is hard to live through these types of events. However, it is the price that a true leader must be willing to pay. It is the price that must be paid for our profession to be known as an honorable one. A profession with honorable people performing one of the most honorable jobs there is.

Chapter 2

The First Amendment Protects Lying?

So, you're telling me a police officer can lie?

If someone had told me when I was in the Wyoming Law Enforcement Academy in 1991 that during my career I would terminate seventy-five employees over thirteen years, and that one day I would actually have to explain to law enforcement officers that lying and having sex on duty would get them fired, I would have laughed. How in the world would it ever be possible to terminate that many employees from a law enforcement agency? Everybody knows that lying and having sex on duty are fatal offenses in a law enforcement career. We are all taught this in the academy, by our field training officers and through our agency's policies.

Like all officers who graduate from the law enforcement academy, I went directly to my agency's field training program. In my career, I have worked for four law enforcement agencies, three city police departments, and one county sheriff's office. I served as a patrol officer, patrol field training officer, patrol supervisor, detective, SWAT team member, SWAT trainer, SWAT supervisor, training supervisor, and finally as Spokane County Sheriff. There has always been one constant: Thou Shall Not Lie. If you do, you are gone.

I remember telling my rookies, "Look, you're going to make mistakes, some bigger than others. My job is to make sure you learn from those mistakes and, better yet, catch them before they happen. You can survive even big mistakes, as long as they are not illegal or done with malicious intent, on one condition: TELL THE TRUTH. If you lie, there is nothing anyone can, or will, do for you. You will be gone."

Or so I thought.

You are probably thinking, "How does one start with one overturned termination and ultimately end up trying to change state law?"

Simple. The rules and values we live by are dying. Accountability and taking responsibility are dying concepts. Holding people accountable became too risky for leaders because people might stop liking you.

Set high standards and hold everyone to them, especially yourself.

Unless you want to terminate a lot of people or leave a mess for your replacement to fix, you must set high standards and unflinchingly uphold those standards. Any agency that does not uphold its standards will create an environment in which its employees go down the continuum of compromise.

Leadership moment:
Set high standards and hold everyone to them, especially yourself.

Dr. Kevin M. Gilmartin aptly describes the "continuum of compromise" in his book, Emotional Survival for Law Enforcement: A Guide for Officers and Their Families. Simply stated, the continuum of compromise appears when folks start breaking small rules. They start down a slippery slope, which can eventually result in breaking big rules or even the law.

With this in mind, to avoid the continuum of compromise, an organization must:

1. Set high standards based on strong values;
2. Train to those standards, keeping its values in mind;
3. Reinforce those standards/values; and
4. Hold people accountable to those standards and never compromise.

An organization must adopt these four rules if it wishes to prevent its members and even the organization as a whole from making choices that will put them on a path toward the continuum of compromise.

An organization's honor, reputation, and public trust start and stop with the values its leadership hold to be important and their willingness to uphold those values as standards. Do your own research. Look at agencies, units, businesses, organizations, and other groups with strong values, and you will find they set high standards/values and demand their members live by them. You'll also find that they are typically the best in their fields. These are not just good organizations; they are great organizations. Try lying as a United States Special Forces trainee or operator. You're done. End of story. Your peers will see to it.

Some of you may be thinking, "Come on. These are police officers. They were hired because they were found to have high character." For any LEO (law enforcement officer) reading this, change the "they" to "we."

For the most part, you are right. We do hire highly motivated people who have very high values and character and who idealistically want to serve and protect their communities. Most agencies want to think they are hiring people with these qualities.

How is it that these bright, shiny, new recruits turn into a detective who exposes his penis to a barista?

We will explore that as we continue our journey.

There was a point in 2009, during my early years as Sheriff, when I was really down about all the disciplinary issues I was facing. I called my jail captain over for a sit down. I asked him to list all the disciplinary issues involving staff we had faced that year, including those we were currently investigating in the jail. I wanted to compare them to a list of the disciplinary issues I was facing on the law enforcement side of the house. Be careful what you ask for.

As I was typing away, John flipped his legal-size notebook over and started down another page. I stopped and asked just him how many he had. "Over thirty," he answered. That's not what I needed. Remember I said I was a little down and concerned about disciplinary issues to start with. By the time he finished telling me about each and every case, let's just say I was somewhere in the emotional basement.

Why? Remember our discussion in the first chapter: Never terminate someone unless you are looking them in the eye. Well, unless you have no soul, each and every termination takes a part of your soul with it. I've always said the day it no longer bothers me to terminate someone is the day I need to go.

Many of the policy and law violations on our lists had rsulted in terminations. The quiet majority was relieved when these bad actors were terminated, while the loud minority within the agency thought I was the dark lord for terminating these folks.

And that minority began making my life a little more complicated by working to get rid of me. The strange thing is that most of those who were screaming at me the loudest were, at the same time, telling me I needed to hold more people accountable.

I know, I know, it made my head hurt too.

You're probably thinking, "Wait, they wanted you to hold bad actors accountable, but at the same time, they were trying to get rid of you?"

Yes, they wanted people held accountable, but not that accountable.

This is how one of them explained it to me. "Look, it could be me who gets fired next if I were to do something similar to what they did."

When I heard this, my answer was always, "Are you planning on doing something like that?" Their answer was always no.

No joke. This was the logic. Hold us accountable, but not that accountable. If the last bit wasn't surreal enough, the next one will really have you saying, "Come again?" When I talked one-on-one with some of the folks who hated me for my stance of holding people accountable, they would say, "Sheriff, good job. That one needed to go."

One of these people was a sergeant in the jail who worked with a group of officers that not only wanted me gone—they wanted my head on a pole. She told her peers something to the effect of, "Ozzie never fired anyone who should not have been fired." Yes, she was one of those who wanted me gone. If you're trying to wrap your head around this, don't. I never could.

Leadership moment:

Good folks don't want to work with bad folks.

Good folks don't want to work with bad folks.

Good leaders know that good people don't want to work with bad people. People want to be held accountable, and they expect bad actors to be held accountable. You'll know you have a healthy agency when the troops come to you about the bad actors instead of you finding out another way. I was blessed in this respect; most of the seventy-five terminations were a result of peers reporting on their coworkers. If good people see that you will deal with the problems, they will help you take care of the problem.

Don't let your good employees down by not dealing with the employee who is making you all look bad!

If you fail in this area, your good employees will do one of three things: leave, shut down (why should I bust my butt when Lee gets paid as much as I do to do nothing?), or bury their heads and hope they don't get caught up in the coming lawsuits.

To those in law enforcement who are reading this book, remember that when a police officer does something bad, every police officer in the nation wears the shame. Don't believe me? Then you haven't been watching the news lately. Even when police officers do it right, if the situation is controversial in any way, all police officers take the public beating.

So again, what were the existing factors that resulted in my terminating seventy-five employees in thirteen years? Remember what I said happens to organizations when leadership fails to consistently and unflinchingly uphold standards?

The following example will give you a good indication as to why I found myself in such a mess.

I was the Spokane County Deputy Sheriff's Association (DSA) union president for five years. One day I had a conversation with the Sheriff that went along these lines:

Me: Sheriff, there is a rumor that a supervisor violated policy and that the incident is being covered up.

Sheriff: Ozzie, that's not true. There was no policy violation

Me: So you're saying that none of this is true.

Sheriff: Absolutely not true.

Me: Okay, I'll go back and tell everyone that the rumor is not true and to knock it off.

When this rumor started going around, several deputies approached me wanting to know what I was going to do about it. After all, I was their union president. I went to the Sheriff in hopes of killing the rumor. As mentioned above, the Sheriff assured me that the rumor was false, so I went back to the troops and told them that the Sheriff was adamant that this was gossip. I also told them to stop rumormongering.

Silly me. About six months later, the Sheriff and I would have another conversation similar to the first.

Me: "Sheriff, about six months ago you told me that the supervisor had not violated policy. Now we learn that he had. I trusted you. I went back to the troops and told them that the old man said the rumor was not true. So now they want to know if I was lying to them or if you were lying to them, and we both know that I only told them what you told me."

Sheriff: Yes, he did violate policy. I didn't want to hurt his career or humiliate him, so it was kept quiet. He has served for nearly thirty years, he's a supervisor, and I didn't want to have him embarrassed."

More likely, the Sheriff didn't want to stand in front of the cameras and explain this one. In his mind, it would make him look bad. In reality, it makes everyone who wears a badge look bad when one of us goes off the rails.

"Sheriff, you've really hurt yourself with this one. You lied. You lied to me, and worse, you lied to your deputies. You've proven to them that the higher the rank, the more you are protected. I'll never stand up for you again because I can't trust you. And worse for everyone, your agency no longer trusts you."

Leaders must have higher standards than anyone else in the organization.

As a leader, you must live by standards that set the bar for the entire organization. Unless you want to face years of trying to fix a mess like the one I inherited, uphold your standards and hold yourself and your leaders to even higher standards than everyone else.

When I became Sheriff, it was important to me that disciplinary issues were dealt with in a fair and consistent manner.

Since it would be nearly impossible to terminate someone for getting a DUI, I decided that if a deputy were to get a DUI, they would receive a forty-hour suspension. Then, if they were to get another one, they would be terminated.

On the other hand, if a supervisor (detective/corporal/sergeant/lieutenant) were to get a DUI, they would get an eighty-hour suspension and if they were get another, they would be terminated. A member of my command staff with one DUI would be demoted and receive an eighty-hour suspension, and then be terminated in the case of a second DUI. What do you think they thought of that?

"Sheriff, this isn't fair. We are lieutenants, and we shouldn't be treated differently. We have to make the hard decisions, so we shouldn't be held to a higher standard. We've done our time."

Leadership moment:

Leaders must have higher standards than anyone else in the organization.

"No lieutenant, that is why you should be held to a higher standard. Your job is to lead and uphold our standards. It is your job to be a role model to our young deputies."

Leaders lead by example.

I know that as a leader, I can't expect my subordinates to follow the rules if I and my leaders are out breaking those same rules. Leaders lead by example and need to hold themselves to the highest of standards. As a leader, under no circumstances should you cover things up or lie to your folks. The day a leader loses the trust of the organization is the day that leader needs to leave.

The Washington State Supreme Court played a key role in the downfall of Washington State's standards. And they did it while hiding behind the First Amendment. The day I learned that lying was protected speech was the day I knew America was on the path to losing its values. Growing up, I remember being told multiple times about a boy who admitted to chopping down a cherry tree (George Washington) and a guy named Honest Abe (Abraham Lincoln). As a nation, we were once taught the importance of truth.

Leadership moment:
Leaders lead by example.

Case #1:

Rickert v. State Public Disclosure Commission, October 4, 2007

In 2002, Ms. Rickert challenged incumbent Senator Tim Sheldon in the election for state senator from Washington's 35th Legislative District. During the campaign, Ms. Rickert sponsored a mailing that included a brochure comparing her positions to those of Senator Sheldon. In part, the brochure stated that Ms. Rickert "[s]upports social services for the most vulnerable of the state's citizens." By way of comparison, the brochure stated that Senator Sheldon "voted to close a facility for the developmentally challenged in his district." In response to the latter statement, Senator Sheldon filed a complaint with the Public Disclosure Commission (PDC).

The Majority's ruling, supported by Justices: Gerry L. Alexander, Charles W. Johnson, Richard B. Sanders, Susan Owens, James M. Johnson.

In the case at bar, Ms. Rickert made knowingly false or reckless statements about Senator Sheldon, a man with an outstanding reputation. Senator Sheldon and his (many) supporters responded to Ms. Rickert's false statements with the truth. As a consequence, Ms. Rickert's statements appear to have had little negative impact on Senator Sheldon's successful campaign and may even have increased his vote (noting that "Senator Sheldon was reelected by approximately 79 percent of the vote."). Were there injury to Senator Sheldon's reputation, compensation would be available through a defamation action. As it is, Ms. Rickert was singled out by the PDC for punishment, six months after the election, based on statements that had no apparent impact on the government interests allegedly furthered by the statute. That the statute may be applied in such a manner proves that it is fatally flawed under the First Amendment.

There can be no doubt that false personal attacks are too common in political campaigns, with wide-ranging detrimental consequences. However, government censorship is not a constitutionally permitted remedy. We hold that this statute, which allows a government agency to censor political speech, is unconstitutional and affirm the decision of the Court of Appeals.

For the dissent, led by Justice Barbara Madsen and joined by Justices Tom Chambers, Mary Fairhurst and Bobbe Bridge.

Unfortunately, the majority's decision is an invitation to lie with impunity. The majority opinion advances the efforts of those who would turn political campaigns into contests of the best stratagems of lies and deceit, to the end that honest discourse and honest candidates are lost in the maelstrom. The majority does no service to the people of Washington when it turns the First Amendment into a shield for the "unscrupulous and skillful" liar to use knowingly false statements as an "effective political tool" in election campaigns. It is little wonder that so many view political campaigns with distrust and cynicism.

As I stated earlier, all thirty-eight of the other sheriffs in the State of Washington joined me in trying to pass legislation stating that police officers should not lie or break the law while on duty. Why do we even need a law like that? The reason starts with two Washington State Supreme Court cases.

On October 4, 2007, the Washington State Supreme Court handed down a decision in the matter of Rickert v. Public Disclosure Commission. This decision would place law enforcement integrity, and society in general, on the continuum of compromise. I include most of the official decision here to show the reasoning the justices used to support lying.

Essentially, the decision by the majority of the justices in this case made lying protected speech under the First Amendment. Those justices who disagreed stated that this decision turned the First Amendment "into a shield for the 'unscrupulous and skillful' liar." It means that liars can get away with any lie they want to tell, even if it's a public lie meant to destroy the reputation of someone else.

I agree with the dissenting justices and take their stance one step further. In today's society, this decision has made it nearly impossible to convince good people to run for political office. Why would anyone who values their reputation run for office and risk their reputation by subjecting themselves to having untruths said about them, all in the name of politics?

In the Rickert case, the majority was wrong, especially in today's social media-driven world. The majority is naïve in thinking that the citizenry will have the desire or ability to ferret out the truth, particularly in political campaigns like the one mentioned above.

All it takes is a lie to be launched on Facebook, and within minutes, the damage that is done causes a reputation to be ruined beyond repair. Most people have no concept of the amount of time, energy, and money the offended candidate must expend in order to get their campaign back on track

and save their reputation. I wonder if the fact that the Washington State Supreme Court justices are elected had anything to do with the majority's decision. This begs the question about the integrity of their own campaigns.

With this one decision, lying became protected speech, and the continuum of compromise was set into motion for an entire state.

Case #2:

Kitsap County Deputy Sheriff's Guild v. Kitsap County, June 26, 2007

The next Washington State Supreme Court case to advance the continuum of compromise regarding lying was between Kitsap County (just west of Seattle) and the sheriff's union there.

The facts of the case are somewhat lengthy. Suffice to say that the case revolved around a Kitsap County Deputy who had been caught in several falsehoods and was terminated for untruthfulness. The Kitsap County Deputy Sheriff's Guild fought the termination, and an arbitrator gave the deputy his job back. Sheriff Steve Boyer appealed the case, and the Washington State Supreme Court ultimately heard it. The Court stated:

> The arbitrator held that the County met six of the seven elements of just cause, including showing that the deputy had been untruthful, but that the County had failed to show that "the degree of discipline administered was reasonably related to the seriousness of the proven offenses.

Remember folks, the deputy was terminated for lying. Untruthfulness is one of the most serious offenses a deputy can commit.

Kitsap County would point to the Brady Rule as one of their main arguments on why the Court should overturn the arbitrator's judgment.

Definition of Brady Rule:

The Brady Rule, named after Brady v. Maryland, 373 U.S. 83 (1963), requires prosecutors to disclose materially exculpatory evidence in the government's possession to the defense. Exculpatory evidence can include information about law enforcement officers, including that they lied in the course of their official duties. Law enforcement officers who find themselves on a Brady list may be unable to testify effectively in court, which is one of the essential functions of a police officer.

In response to the County's position, the Court stated:

Leadership moment: Integrity is the foundation of honor. Without integrity, you have no honor.

The County contends that the Brady rule—which requires prosecutors to disclose exculpatory evidence—exemplifies a public policy against reinstatement of police officers found to be untruthful. The County argues that prosecutors would have to disclose [redacted] record of dishonesty in any criminal proceedings where [redacted] served as a witness. However, even if that were true, it would not be sufficient to vacate the arbitration decision because it does not constitute an explicit, well defined, and dominant public policy prohibiting [redacted] reinstatement. The cases requiring disclosure of an officer's history of untruthfulness have not commented on whether such an officer could continue to be employed. As a result, there is no explicit (or even implicit) statement regarding the continued employment of an officer found to be untruthful. Further, even if Brady case law constituted a public policy against reinstatement of an officer found to be dishonest, it provides no guidance regarding what level of dishonesty would prohibit reinstatement. The Brady rule provides neither an explicit nor a well-defined public policy against reinstating an officer found to be untruthful. As such, the Brady rule does not meet the exacting requirements necessary to void an arbitration award on public policy grounds. The public policy discussed in the dissent fails to meet the strict standard of "explicit, well defined, and dominant." RCW 41.14.110 does require that deputy sheriffs serve only during good behavior but provides dismissal as one option among many, including suspension, demotion, or deprivation of vacation privileges.

Okay, who caught it? Did you note that the Washington State Supreme Court went down the "how big of a lie was it" path? They said that "even if Brady case law constituted a public policy against reinstatement of an officer found to be dishonest, it provides no guidance regarding what level of dishonesty would prohibit reinstatement."

I've lost count of how many times I've had to debate the question, "What exactly is a lie?" I've heard the "bell curve of lies" theory, which states that lies should be weighed on a bell curve, or on a "color chart of lies" ranging from white to gray to obsidian black.

I've been asked, "Sheriff, just how big of a lie was it?" by a County Commissioner in a discussion concerning a deputy's termination. My answer was, "I don't know, Commissioner. It was a lie, and he is a deputy."

In law enforcement, we don't get to lie. Integrity is the foundation of honor. Without integrity, you have no honor.

Integrity is the foundation of honor.
Without integrity, you have no honor.

I bet if you asked any kindergartener what a lie is, they can tell you. It's not telling the truth. Simple as that.

The Court's decision on the Kitsap County case:

CONCLUSION

The arbitrator's decision does not violate an explicit, well defined, and dominant public policy; therefore, we reverse the Court of Appeals and reinstate the arbitrator's decision. The County appropriately returned [redacted] to duty on April 11, 2005, upon passage of fitness-for-duty exams, so no retroactive pay is required.

In simple terms, the Washington State Supreme Court actually stated two things. First, arbitration decisions are final; and second, there is no "well defined, and dominant public policy" preventing a law enforcement officer in the State of Washington from lying.

I can't tell you how frustrating it is to hear these words from your attorney when you are facing reinstatement of a corrupt officer: "Sheriff, it is nearly impossible to appeal this arbitration decision. The Court was clear that an arbitrator's decision is final."

The Court says:

Reviewing an arbitration decision for mistakes of law or fact would call into question the finality of arbitration decisions and undermine alternative dispute resolution. Further, a more extensive review of arbitration decisions would weaken the value of bargained for, binding arbitration and could damage the freedom of contract (holding that "[w]hen parties voluntarily submit to binding arbitration, they generally believe that they are trading their right to appeal an arbitration award for a relatively speedy and inexpensive resolution to their dispute").

Under what conditions will the Court hear an appeal of an arbitration decision? Only when the arbitration decision violates public policy. Per the Court:

> Nonetheless, federal courts and many other state courts have held that—like any other contract—an arbitration decision arising out of a collective bargaining agreement can be vacated if it violates public policy.

Good luck trying to get there.

You're probably thinking, "Wait Sheriff Ozzie, a police officer lying isn't against public policy?"

Nope.

All of the police officers who are not from the State of Washington are most likely wanting to scream "B.S.!" right now. Remember, you can make big mistakes and survive them as long as you don't lie. I learned in the academy that lying was a fatal sin for a police officer. Not to mention all the places in Washington State law that says lying is not acceptable. This is why most law enforcement officers, especially those from outside the State of Washington, are amazed when they learn about the Court's ruling.

If neither of these cases could establish a "clearly defined and dominant public policy," then what in the Court's eyes would? Some of you are likely asking, "How could the Supreme Court of the State of Washington get this so wrong?"

I will refer you back to the Rickert case, where the Court protected lying as free speech, and I will also remind you that the justices on the Washington State Supreme Court are elected, meaning they need money for re-election. And who has a large war chest ready to be used to elect those who are friendly to their cause?

The unions.

Doubt me? You won't after you finish this book.

After the Kitsap County case, the Washington Association of Sheriffs and Police Chiefs (WASPC) sprang into action. In 2010, we tried to get new legislation passed: Senate Bill 6590.

As of February 5, 2010

Title: An act relating to law enforcement officer conduct

Brief Description: Requiring law enforcement officers to be honest and truthful.

Summary of Bill: A new public policy is created which states that a law enforcement officer should be honest and truthful. Arbitrators cannot overturn the decision of an employer to terminate a law enforcement officer for engaging in dishonest acts unless the arbitrator finds that the law enforcement officer was not dishonest or untruthful. A new section is added which imposes this requirement on terminations of police officers by the Washington Criminal Justice Training Commission. The Commission provides programs and standards for training criminal justice personnel.

PRO: It is paramount that officers be honest and truthful in the exercise of their duties. Honesty is the foundation of an officer's authority. This standard should be upheld by sheriffs or police chiefs, not by a private arbitrator who has no public accountability. Search warrants and arrests are based on an officer's sworn testimony. Officers must testify in court and are often the prosecutor's chief witness. An officer who has engaged in dishonesty could jeopardize successful prosecutions of those accused of committing crimes. A clear statement must be sent to the public that officers are expected to be honest and truthful while carrying out their official duties.

CON: The public should have an expectation that police officers be honest. However, the bill may supersede and impede the collective bargaining agreement, thus calling into question its legality. It is important to preserve the contractual obligation, agreed to by both line officers and management, that disputed disciplinary actions be decided by an arbitrator. This bill mandates a certain disciplinary outcome which weakens the arbitrator's power to decide issues arising under a collective bargaining agreement. Sheriffs and police chiefs should be held to the same standards of honesty and truthfulness as line officers.

Persons Testifying:

PRO: Don Pierce, Washington Association of Sheriffs and Police Chiefs (WASPC); Sheriff Mike Harum, Chelan County Sheriff, WASPC, Washington Association of County Officials; Anne Kirkpatrick, Chief of Police, Spokane Police Department; Sheriff Sue Rahr, King County Sheriff.

CON: Rick Jensen, Tom Pillow, Washington State Patrol Troopers Association; Bill Hanson, Washington State Fraternal Order of Police; Anna Jancewicz, Teamsters Union, Local 117

Seems pretty straightforward and reasonable, right? "Arbitrators cannot overturn the decision of an employer to terminate a law enforcement officer for engaging in dishonest acts unless the arbitrator finds that the law enforcement officer was not dishonest or untruthful." Who could have a problem with making sure law enforcement officers tell the truth?

Ask Chelan County Sheriff Mike Harum, who lost his election in 2010, and Police Chief Anne Kirkpatrick, who was hit with a vote of no confidence in April of 2010. Both happened as a result of testifying and leading the push for this bill.

The unions went crazy and beat the legislature into submission. They lobbied and pressured the legislature unrelentingly to stop SB 6590. They painted the bill as an attack on the very foundations of collective bargaining. They claimed that, "the bill may supersede and impede the collective bargaining agreement, thus calling into question its legality. It is important to preserve the contractual obligation, agreed to by both line officers and management, that disputed disciplinary actions be decided by an arbitrator. This bill mandates a certain disciplinary outcome which weakens the arbitrator's power to decide issues arising under a collective bargaining agreement. Sheriffs and police chiefs should be held to the same standards of honesty and truthfulness as line officers."

Really?

None of what you read above is remotely factual, and it will not be the last time you read such union propaganda in this book. Someone needed to tell them that sheriffs and chiefs are held to higher standards than line staff, and, frankly, can be removed not for their own errors, but for the errors of those they lead. Doubt me? Ask the former Chief of Chicago, or, for that matter, any chief or sheriff that has had a bad officer-involved shooting take place on their watch.

How did it all play out?

The unions won. WASPC had its head handed back, and we ended up with a very watered-down state law that basically states we will obey our oath and follow our policies. The trouble is that while the law states we must follow policy, very few policies state that if you lie, you get terminated. Why? Because the unions will never allow such language to be placed in a contract.

The law we ended up with reads, "It is the policy of the state of Washington that all commissioned, appointed, and elected law enforcement personnel comply with their oath of office and agency policies regarding the duty to be truthful and honest in the conduct of their official business."

A little different than the proposed language the SB 6590 originally intended: "Arbitrators cannot overturn the decision of an employer to terminate a law enforcement officer for engaging in dishonest acts unless the arbitrator finds that the law enforcement officer was not dishonest or untruthful."

The end result? Arbitrators can still overturn the decision of a sheriff or chief to terminate someone who lies. Nowhere in the new law does it state or establish a "clearly defined and well established policy" that a police officer should not lie. It is void of the word "untruthfulness."

Little did the sheriffs and chiefs realize that this was just round one in the fight to uphold the standards and honor of our profession. Round one saw a sheriff lose his job and a police chief's career be so damaged that it would take her seven years to repair it. In all respects, the unions won and took their pound of flesh from those who dared to hold them accountable.

In chapter three, you will learn why I fought round two in 2013 and round three in 2014 in an effort to accomplish what should have been finished in the first round. Two arbitration rulings overturning my terminations of a deputy and a corrections officer resulted in my continued efforts to once again change state law. In 2013, a union lobbyist threatened me by saying, "Sheriff, you've pissed us off. If you don't back down now, we're coming after you."

And they did.

Sometimes leaders have to take a stand, even if it means "pissing someone off" who can make your life hell, or even end your career.

A true leader knows that your personal safety and comfort come last, and that the honor of your community and profession comes first. Upholding one's standards comes with a price. Sometimes leaders have to take a stand, even if it means facing the dark reality of your own professional demise. To all would-be leaders, decide now if you are willing to pay that price. And know that it is a price that may cost your job and more. This is the price of honor.

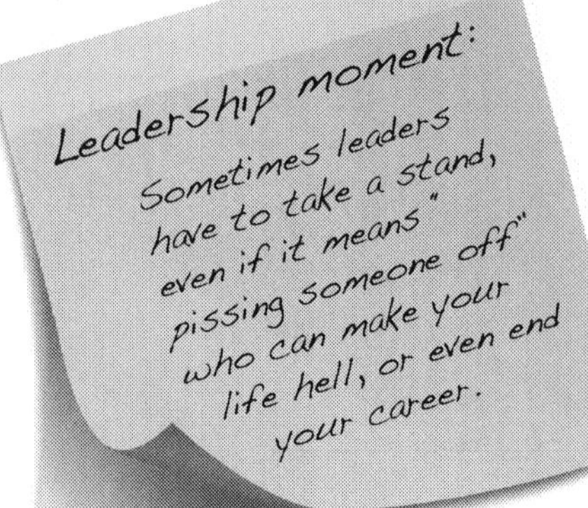

Chapter 3

The Fatal Flaw

This is a bad character trait in anyone.
It is a potentially fatal flaw in a law enforcement official.

In the last chapter, we covered how the Washington State Supreme Court began the erosion of values once thought to be sacred. The Supreme Court's decisions ultimately set the stage for two arbitration decisions covered in this chapter. When the values that define a country, profession, organization, or individual are no longer valued, respected, or upheld, the resulting collapse will rock that entity to its core, if not wipe it out of existence. I fear this is the path upon which we now travel.

It is important for you to understand that both of the employees discussed in this and the next chapter were terminated and were reinstated as a result of arbitration decisions. This means I fired them, they fought their terminations with the help of the union, they were given their jobs back by an arbitrator, and I was forced to give them their jobs back. These arbitration decisions were seminal in my realization that the system truly was broken. When you have arbitrators that say, "Sheriff, you did your job. You didn't violate any labor laws. You proved that they did these things, but we are still going to give them their jobs back," there is something wrong.

Termination and Arbitration Decision #1

The first arbitration decision we will explore finds us dealing with a young deputy who thought his peers would find his actions funny. Let's call him Deputy Dave. I will summarize three incidents involving this deputy that led to his termination.

The amazing thing about this case was Deputy Dave's background. He was hired in August 2007 and graduated from the academy in December of that year. He did very well, graduating with the highest academic score and best overall rating in his class. He obtained his MBA through a well-respected university while working patrol on the night shift. After getting hired, he had a relatively clean disciplinary history up until September 2010. At least, that was how things appeared.

Deputy Dave sounds like the type of hard charger any agency would want, right? For anyone wanting to be a police officer or any young police officer reading this, beware of arrogance. It is poison to law enforcement officers. For any supervisors, this example is what failure to supervise or hold people accountable for minor flaws will blossom into. Failure to take care of the little things results in out of control behavior. Behavior that will destroy your organization if left unchecked.

Failure to take care of the little things will grow into 900-pound gorillas that will beat you and your organization into the dirt.

I can't tell you how many times I've heard a supervisor or peer of someone under investigation say, "Sheriff, we saw it coming."

Well, if you saw it coming, what did you do to stop it? Leaders have the responsibility to identify shortcomings or minor violations and deal with them before they become major issues. Most terminations can be avoided if someone would step in and correct the course the employee is on. If we fail to do so, the continuum of compromise will take hold.

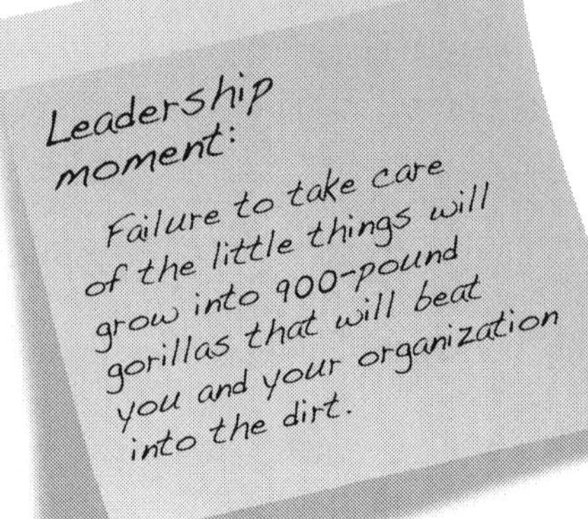

Leaders, this is your responsibility. Line staff, it is also yours. A friend does not let a friend self-destruct. And if the person isn't your friend, a law enforcement officer does not let another law enforcement officer self-destruct, taking the agency and possibly the profession with them. Do us all a favor: Step up and lead.

Termination #1

Incident 1

Deputy Dave's problems didn't start in August of 2010, just three short years from his date of hire. No, the signs should have been noticed in 2009, when he stopped a female driver after she pulled out of the parking lot of a bar on December 13, 2009. What violation did she commit? Not having a license plate light.

Let's refer to this young lady as Sharon. Sharon was driving with a suspended license. After her vehicle and purse were searched by Deputy Dave, marijuana was found. Sharon was arrested for DWLS (driving with license suspended) and PCS Marijuana (possession-controlled substance).

While he was booking her into jail, Deputy Dave decided to look through Sharon's cell phone. Sharon would later state that the deputy found text messages and nude pictures of her on the phone and showed them to other Sheriff's Office personnel that night. If that wasn't bad enough, Dave called her a "drug smuggling prostitute."

These actions revealed issues with Deputy Dave's character. I have a simple rule in life that I have found to be a near absolute: If an employee has a character issue, terminate them. You can't fix bad character. It will always come back.

Simple rule, you cannot fix character. You will always see a repeat offense from those with character issues.

Leadership moment:

Simple rule, you cannot fix character. You will always see a repeat offense from those with character issues.

Deputy Dave's conduct that night required an internal investigation. Sharon's attorney requested video footage from the jail relating to the night of her booking, names of Sheriff's Office personnel on duty that night, and cell phone records.

I have to sidetrack us for a moment here. There was a major issue with the internal investigation concerning this event. The supervisor in charge of our internal affairs unit had failed to collect some information and had stated in his report that he had collected the information. This was not the first incident that he had committed this type of "error", and he had been counseled concerning this type of activity. As a result, I told him that if he ever ended up in front of me for suspicion of untruthfulness again, he would be immediately terminated regardless of his rank, years of service, or the thoughts of my legal advisor. Why wasn't he terminated? Remember those court cases I mentioned in chapter two? Here is how the scenario concerning this supervisor played out:

My attorney: Look, this supervisor has thirty+ years with the agency, a fairly clean record, and good work history. No arbitrator will uphold a termination for lying involving someone with this work history.

Me: But he wasn't truthful. And this isn't the first time we've talked to him about this.

Leadership moment:

Sometimes it is better to follow your gut instead of listening to attorneys.

Attorney: Sheriff, you know what the Court has said about lying.

Me: Okay, okay, I get it. It's okay to lie in the State of Washington. But I'm telling you right now, if he comes before me again because he has lied, he is done, and there is nothing you or anyone else can say that will change my mind. Don't say it. I know he'll sue us. That's okay, that's why I have you. Your job is to defend my actions. Don't say it. I know my actions have to be reasonable. I believe a jury would find them to be very reasonable.

Sometimes it is better to follow your gut instead of listening to attorneys.

For you leaders involved in situations that require legal advice, take note

that sometimes it is better to follow your gut instead of listening to your attorney. Their job is to defend your actions. Your job is to make sure you've done your job well enough so they can defend your actions.

Because the above-mentioned supervisor did not do his job, I was unable to catch the character flaw in time to correct Deputy Dave. The 2009 traffic stop involving Sharon was not fully investigated until November of 2010, when the same attorney contacted the Sheriff's Office stating he had two potential civil rights violations concerning Dave, one of which concerned Sharon.

Incident 2

On August 29, 2010, Deputy Dave made another traffic stop, which ultimately led to the female driver's car being impounded and placed in the Sheriff's Office parking lot. Let's call this driver Barbara.

Before impounding the car, Dave decided to write Barbara a citation listing seven violations for faulty equipment on her vehicle. Why? Because she told him that the police frequently stopped her, then sarcastically said that she did not get any tickets although she "wished" she had been given tickets. Her sarcasm angered Dave so much that he made sure she received a ticket, several tickets.

As if seven violations weren't bad enough, he would later mail Barbara another citation listing two more violations that he had forgotten to add during the stop. So, he issued her nine total equipment violations because he felt she had impugned his reputation and integrity by stating that she never got tickets.

Once the vehicle was at the Sheriff's Office parking lot, Deputy Dave searched the vehicle based on a search warrant. This is where a bad situation became a really bad situation.

While searching the worn-out truck, which was worth absolutely nothing except maybe as scrap (for the law enforcement officers reading this, yes, he was going to try to seize the vehicle and sell it), Dave found a Nazi bandana. He took it, tore holes in it, and strung it up on the antenna like a flag. He then found a fixed-blade knife with a brass knuckle handle. He took the knife and forced it into passenger side seat up to its hilt. When he was asked why he did these things, he stated that he thought the guys in our investigative support unit would find them funny.

You think anyone was laughing when Barbara came to claim her vehicle? Nope. Imagine her reaction when she saw the Nazi bandana flag on her antenna and the illegal knife stuck in the passenger seat of her vehicle. She asked the deputy helping her recover her vehicle if we were trying to send her a message.

You may be thinking, "Wait Sheriff Ozzie, the vehicle had been seized for confiscation. How did she get it back?"

Because there is a process that such a confiscation has to go through, and

that vehicle was never going to be confiscated due to its condition. So yes, we returned the vehicle, and yes, she was very upset about the damage. But she was more upset that her law enforcement agency had done this to her vehicle.

See how that works, folks? For her, it went from one deputy committing these crimes against her to her whole law enforcement agency committing them. That is how it works. When an officer breaks the law or does something that brings dishonor to the badge, everyone who wears a badge wears that dishonor.

Anytime a law enforcement officer breaks the law or does something that brings dishonor to the badge, everyone who wears a badge wears that dishonor.

Leadership moment:
Anytime a law enforcement officer breaks the law or does something that brings dishonor to the badge, everyone who wears a badge wears that dishonor.

It might be hard to sympathize with Barbara, knowing some of the details, but think about it this way. Say you get pulled over and for some reason your vehicle is seized and hauled to the Sheriff's Office lot. You are left by the side of the road alone because the officer didn't like the way you talked them. When you finally get your vehicle back, there is a knife sticking out of the seat, and something from inside the vehicle is now damaged and prominently displayed on the antenna. Do you see the slippery slope? Would you trust any police officer again?

The big problem was that Deputy Dave was under the supervision of a detective when he was searching the vehicle. The supervising detective should have stopped Dave and told him that that type of behavior was unacceptable. Had he done so, neither the bandana nor the seat would have been damaged. Supervisors need to do their jobs, even when it is uncomfortable. Especially when it is uncomfortable.

Supervisors need to do their jobs, even when it is uncomfortable.

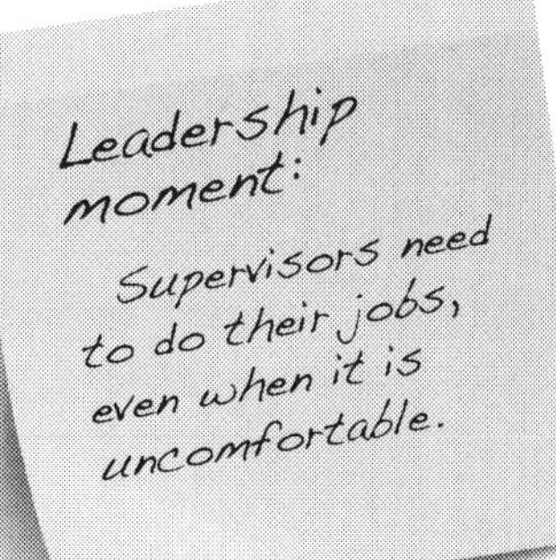

There is a drought of leadership today, especially in law enforcement.

No one wants to hold leadership positions anymore. Why? Because no one wants to be that guy or gal who has to hold someone else accountable. Doing so makes people upset and angry, and they may not like you anymore. Humans are social animals. They like to be liked. When you suddenly become the person responsible for holding people accountable, those you thought to be your friends can suddenly turn on you. Especially if the agency had let its standards slip. Leadership is lonely, and the higher up you go, the lonelier it gets.

It has been my experience that good employees really want to be held accountable, and it is only the vocal minority that cry the loudest about being held accountable. When folks learn that you are serious about upholding values and standards, they tend to start influencing bad employees to get onboard.

A little moral to the leadership moment: Upholding your agency's values and standards will result in the good troops eventually having your back, but you will think the world is against you until the day those good troops finally step forward.

Incident 3

During the internal investigation into the incident involving Barbara, another incident was discovered. This time we learned that Deputy Dave had stopped a woman who was speeding. Let's call her Debbie. Deputy Dave searched Debbie's vehicle after arresting her for DWLS (driving without a license). He found two prescription bottles in her purse. One of the bottles was empty and had a label showing a prescription for Hydrocodone with Debbie's name on it. The other was an unmarked bottle containing ten Hydrocodone pills. The deputy seized the bottles and decided to tow her car, despite the fact that her father had come to the scene to take possession of it. Debbie was released with the citation.

What did Deputy Dave do with the seized narcotics, you ask? Well, he put them in his unsecured mailbox in an unsecured portion of our precinct. The charges against Debbie were ultimately dismissed, and she contacted the police evidence room to retrieve her Hydrocodone pills, which she did have a prescription for. She was told that the evidence room did not have any record of her pills ever being placed on evidence.

Her next stop? You guessed it. The Sheriff's Office. We checked the deputy's report and found no mention of the pills being confiscated or placed into evidence. During an interview, Deputy Dave said the pills were in his mailbox.

Yes, he actually let those Schedule 1 narcotics sit in his mailbox for fifty-two days.

And yes, this is a major violation of policy. Anyone could have taken them. The pills were recovered from his mailbox and returned to Debbie.

Needless to say, I suddenly found myself facing three disciplinary investigations involving the same deputy, and somehow I had to decide the outcomes of these three cases so that the discipline would be progressive and fitting for each violation.

I decided to take the events in the chronological order of their occurrence. The discipline for each event was as follows:

- Debbie: On October 20, 2010, I issued a written reprimand for Improper search/seizure, Failure to maintain chain of custody/evidence, Failure to document official actions in a report, and Conduct Unbecoming. Along with the written reprimand, I ordered that the deputy be put through remedial training concerning the above areas of policy and the law.
- Sharon: On January 20, 2011, I issued discipline consisting of verbal counseling and remedial training addressing pre-textual stops, including application of related court rulings and proper documentation in reports of one's actions.
- Barbara: On January 24, 2011, the deputy was terminated for conduct that was in violation of Sheriff's Office Policy and Procedures, RCW 9A.48.090 Malicious Mischief in the Third Degree and Civil Service law.

It was an amazing journey getting to January 24, 2011. During the early part of the investigation into the matter involving Barbara, the president of the deputy's union (DSA) and vice president told me that this thing with Deputy Dave was not as bad as it appeared. They told me that when Dave found the knife, he picked it up, looked at it, and threw it back into the vehicle, resulting in it sticking in the seat.

I asked them if I had this right: He just threw it back into the vehicle with no intent of it sticking in the seat, and the fact that it stuck into the seat was an unintended consequence. They said I understood them correctly.

"Well, if that is the case, then that is dumb, but not fatal." I told them I would review the internal affairs report when it was complete and if that was the finding, I could see a suspension in his future but not much more.

To this day, I wonder if Deputy Dave had lied to the union or if the union lied to me. I say this based on the following events.

During the investigation, Deputy Dave stated that he had forced the knife into the seat because he thought our investigative support unit would find it funny.

I can tell you the deputies and detectives who worked in that unit did not find it funny when they learned of this statement. On the contrary, they were very angry that anyone would think that they would find such actions funny.

Based on all this evidence, and the fact that he never took responsibility for his actions, he was terminated. Any deputy who is willing to damage private property and not be truthful about it doesn't deserve to wear a badge.

Definition of Loudermill – A Loudermill hearing is a hearing in which the accused employee has their last chance to tell their side of the event and present mitigating evidence. It is also a name clearing hearing.

During both the investigation and Loudermill hearing, Deputy Dave was asked several times how the knife ended up stuck in the seat. Deputy Dave gave an "A, B, or C" answer.

A what kind of answer?

"A, B, or C." Dave stated he either: A. threw the knife back into the truck, causing it to be stuck into the seat; B. threw the knife back into the truck, causing it to stick into the seat, then forced the knife further into the seat (because he had to explain how the knife ended up buried up to its hilt in the seat); or C. stuck the knife into the seat, burying it up to its hilt.

If you are thinking, "Either way, he's not being very truthful," you are right. Remember those two Supreme Court cases? This is what I knew going into the Loudermill hearing on January 24, 2011.

I again asked during the hearing how the knife ended up in the seat of the truck. You guessed it. He gave his "A, B, or C" response. I looked at the union vice president and told him that perhaps he needed to step out of the hearing and talk with Dave.

I was expecting the union VP to pull the deputy aside and tell him, "Look, you told us you just threw the knife back into the truck, and that's what we told the old man. You need to come clean here."

Instead, when they came back into the room, I was once again given the "A, B, or C" explanation. I will never understand this move on his or the union's part.

This was his chance to come clean, and it was the union's chance to tell him, "Either come clean or we're done with you." Neither of which happened. Instead, he maintained his multiple-choice answer, and they defended him all the way through the grievance process and through the arbitration process.

In most disciplinary processes involving union collective bargaining, arbitration is the last part of the process. Once violations have been investigated, the facts are put through a "just cause for discipline" matrix. The level of discipline is then handed out. At this point, the employee can file a grievance if they feel mistakes were made in the process, the discipline given was too harsh, or the findings of the investigation were incorrect. If the parties cannot reach a compromise concerning the grievance, either party can ask that the matter go before an arbitrator.

In many respects, it is like taking the matter to trial in the court system. Similar to a judge, the arbitrator hears the case and makes findings based on facts of the case, allegations filed in the plaintiff's grievance, and handling of the disciplinary process. In the State of Washington, it is near impossible to appeal an arbitrator's decision.

Arbitration Decision #1

The Arbitrator noted the following in her decision:

At the outset, I want to address the union argument that the Sheriff's Office "manipulated" the investigations of these matters, to set this up to appear as a progressive discipline leading to termination. I disagree. The situation here—three unrelated complaints being considered at essentially the same time—would present a challenge to any workplace discipline system. The Sheriff's Office made a reasonable effort to evaluate each one on its own merits.

- It was determined that there was probable cause to charge Grievant with Malicious Mischief in the Third Degree, but S3 did not press charges. The Sheriff's conclusion that Grievant violated RCW 9A. 48.090 was established by clear and convincing evidence.
- Grievant testified that he issued the nine infractions in response to S3's comments which he considered a "personal attack on his ethics and integrity." Grievant, however, denies he had any retaliatory intention. An individual charged with retaliation will rarely acknowledge their subjective intent. In my view, however, Grievant's admission that he took the action…comes pretty close to admitting he was "punishing" S3 for her comment. Nothing in this record suggests this action was either routine or appropriate… Grievant's inappropriate action, in response to S3's comment, was retaliatory. Even if it was not considered retaliatory per se, it was, nevertheless, discourteous treatment of the public through excessive, unreasonable and wrongful use of authority in violation of policy.
- The Sheriff has met [the] burden of establishing that Grievant's handling of the Oxycodone was highly irregular, and in violation of multiple policies. One does not have to be a police officer to understand that documentation of official actions – including evidence seizure, and maintaining a chain of custody and chain of evidence - is more than "technical." …The Sheriff established Grievant's guilt.

(NOTE: The term "Grievant" refers to Deputy Dave, and "S3" refers to Barbara, who had the knife stuck into her truck seat.)

In her decision, the arbitrator stated that I had done my job in this matter and had done it well.

You may be thinking, "Okay, Sheriff, the arbitrator found that you proved your case and the deputy did all these bad things. Why did she give his job back?"

Below are some of the reasons she gave in her arbitration decision:

- The finding of an employee's guilt does not necessarily mean the discipline imposed will be upheld. In order to satisfy basic notions of "just cause," discipline must be proportional. This means it "bears some reasonable relation to the seriousness…of the offense."
- The Sheriff argues that S3 was a capital offense which, if considered a first offence, justifies termination; progressive discipline was not required, both due to severity of the conduct and because of Grievant's failure to take true "responsibility."…I have fully considered the briefs as well as relevant portions of the written record. Perhaps, most importantly, I have listened again to the testimony of both Grievant and the Sheriff. I have concluded that Grievant's actions, given the entirety of the relevant circumstances, did not justify his termination.
- I credited Grievant's belief – however misinformed and naïve – that S3 would not see the damage he did to her property. (He never stopped to think that the forfeited property would then belong to Spokane County.) These factors in no way lessen the fact that he engaged in criminal acts…The factors can, and appropriately do, however, impact the justified level of discipline. No criminal activity is "acceptable" but not all criminal activity is the same, and this activity, given the other circumstances, did not support summary termination.
- The absence of the opportunity to improve was, however, part of my concern with the termination decision.
- In deciding to terminate Grievant, the Sheriff articulated several reasons why he did not think Grievant was amenable to corrective action. As discussed below, I am very sympathetic to the Sheriffs concerns. In fact, I am convinced that if Grievant had genuinely and consistently accepted responsibility for his actions and had sincerely acknowledged his obligation to perform consistent with the reasonable standards set by the Sheriff, he likely would not have been terminated. Grievant is more than capable of understanding the policies and laws that necessarily govern the very difficult job of being a Spokane Deputy Sheriff. He must recommit himself to consistently conforming to those policies and laws.
- [T]he record amply demonstrates that Grievant has a hard time truly taking responsibility for his actions. His hearing testimony, unemployment hearing testimony, interviews, and statements demonstrate a strong tendency to blame others…This is a bad character trait in anyone. It is a potentially fatal flaw in a law enforcement official.

Well, there you have it. I know you're thinking, "She found that you did your job. You proved he committed crimes, gave the tickets in retaliation, didn't take responsibility, and blamed others for his actions. She shared your concern that the deputy may not change. She said he 'rationalized' his behavior and called this 'a bad character trait in anyone.' She said, 'It is a potentially fatal flaw in a law enforcement official.' How in the world did she give his job back?"

To this day, I cannot see how the arbitrator came to this decision.

Even now this deputy has not fully accepted responsibility for his actions, and it comes up each time he is due for a specialty job or promotion. He wanted to become a field-training officer recently. How does one let someone with this record train the next generation of deputies? And how does one let someone like this become a supervisor?

That decision is just a gift that keeps on giving.

This decision was itself a *fatal flaw.*

The Return of the Fatal Flaw

During the time this book was being written, this *fatal flaw* would come full circle. In March of 2018, Deputy Dave once again was under criminal and internal investigation. This time for violating the rights of one of our citizens and breaking state law concerning recording of conversations.

The State of Washington is a two-party consent state concerning the recording of conversations, meaning that both parties have to consent to the recording. Deputy Dave not only recorded a conversation without the knowledge of the other party during an investigation, but he did so after being reminded by his sergeant that he needed to get consent to record the conversation.

The case was sent to the County Prosecutor for charges to be filed. The County Prosecutor punted the case to the City of Spokane Prosecutor, who refused to file charges against Deputy Dave. Why? 2018 was an election year for both me and the County Prosecutor. He punted it because he did not want to anger the Deputy Sheriff's Association. As to the City Prosecutor, no one wants to anger the Spokane Police Guild. I hate to say it, but that's how it works, folks. I fully understand the feeling the public has when it comes to police officers not being held accountable. As a law enforcement leader, I share your anger and your frustration. The vast majority of Sheriffs and Chiefs do our best to hold our law enforcement officers accountable, and it is frustrating to have a bad apple returned by an arbitrator or to have charges dismissed when we forward them to the Prosecutor's Office.

The one bright spot in this story came in May of 2019 during the final edit of this book. Despite the union's attorney pulling one of the most underhanded stunts I have ever seen, the arbitrator in this case upheld my termination of Deputy Dave.

Once again, Deputy Dave refused to take responsibility for his actions. Both he and the union threw his sergeant under the bus by trying to paint him as having a poor memory. Deputy Dave and the union claimed that Dave didn't have any conversation with the sergeant concerning recording the statement and that the sergeant's memory was based on a conversation he had with another deputy about the incident. They claimed that the sergeant transferred the other deputy's memory of talking with Deputy Dave about the recording to his own memory. If you're getting that feeling that your head is starting to hurt again, well…I'm not going to go into details concerning that rabbit hole.

Once again, the *fatal flaw* in Deputy Dave's character raised its head, and we now come full circle in his story.

Chapter 4

Jumping Jacks

This administration will not tolerate such behavior because we are to be professional at all times.

The next arbitration decision led to my attempt to change Washington State law. This arbitration decision was possibly more unsettling than the one in the previous chapter, due to the nature of the incident.

This case made me stop saying, "I've seen everything." This is the case that made me question altogether the sanity of unions. It proved to me that both the arbitration system and union representation had gone to the dark side. This case made me lose faith in our federal prosecutorial system. This is when I finally said, "Things have to change."

Termination and Arbitration Decision #2

Christmas Eve, 2010. A corrections deputy at the jail makes a mentally ill inmate on suicide watch strip naked and do jumping jacks. Of course, the deputy had a reason for doing it. He did it as a joke.

What do you think, any civil rights violations here? Any law violations?

The inmate had been seen tearing up his safety blanket earlier that day. Our corrections deputy—let's call him Corrections Deputy Jerry—stated that he wanted to see if the inmate had any pieces of the blanket stashed under his jump suit. He claimed that this is why he had the inmate strip naked.

Why the jumping jacks? Knew you might ask that one.

Corrections Deputy Jerry stated in the investigation that he had the inmate do the jumping jacks to see if any of the blanket pieces or some kind of cutting device that may have been used to cut the blanket up was stashed in his buttocks. Yep, buttocks. I've always said you can't make this stuff up.

Termination #2

In order to help those of you not in law enforcement or corrections understand the severe legal and civil rights implications of this act, I am going to walk you through it:

The law and proper procedures:

1. RCW 10.79.060 Strip, body cavity searches–Legislative intent.
   a) It is the intent of the legislature to establish policies regarding the practice of strip searching persons booked into holding, detention, or local correctional facilities. It is the intent of the legislature to restrict the practice of strip searching and body cavity searching persons booked into holding, detention, or local correctional facilities to those situations where such searches are necessary.
   b) RCW 10.79.070(1) defines "Strip search" as "having a person remove or arrange some or all of his or her clothing so as to permit

an inspection of the genitals, buttocks, anus, or undergarments of the person or breasts of a female person."

c) In order to perform a strip search, you have to have a valid legal reason to do so.

d) In order to perform a strip search, you have to have a supervisor's permission.

   i. In a strip search, a supervisor observes while two corrections deputies handcuff the inmate and inspect his mouth, ears, hair, and the bottom of his feet; they also direct male inmates to lift their genitals, bend over, spread their buttocks, and then cough.

e) If you perform a strip search, there are important forms that have to be filled out before and after and approved by a supervisor.

f) One cannot decide to conduct a strip search without doing all of the above.

The civil rights issues:

1. U.S. Supreme Court ruled in Estelle v. Gamble that ignoring a prisoner's serious medical needs can amount to cruel and unusual punishment, noting that "[a]n inmate must rely on prison authorities to treat his medical needs; if the authorities fail to do so, those needs will not be met. In the worst cases, such a failure may actually produce physical torture or a lingering death."
2. Mentally ill inmates have certain protections that must be maintained.
3. You cannot take advantage of a mentally ill inmate in any way.
4. Officers are responsible to keep inmates safe from each other. They are also obligated to keep inmates safe from themselves. Officers and civilian staff in prisons, jails, and police lock-ups have to deal with the possibility that inmates under their supervision might attempt to take their own lives…Correctional staff members have a moral duty to provide care for inmates and work to prevent suicides.
   a) Suicidal inmates have certain protections and are to be watched very closely to prevent any harm from coming to them.
   b) Mentally ill and suicidal inmates are not to be treated in any fashion which may result in their conditions becoming more aggravated.
   c) Mentally ill and suicidal inmates have a protective status while in jail.

This gives you some idea of how bad the situation really was. The bottom line here is that a mentally ill or suicidal inmate should not be treated in any way that can be determined abusive or demeaning. Our corrections deputy broke every rule concerning strip searches and the treatment of a mentally ill/suicidal inmate.

You are probably wondering if anyone tried to stop him. There were other corrections deputies on the floor, including the field training officer for

Corrections Deputy Jerry. Even though Jerry had been with the Sheriff's Office for twenty years, at the time of this incident, he had been assigned as a training officer because he had been away from the jail for five years on a special assignment.

When asked what happened that Christmas Eve, all of the corrections deputies on the floor stated that they were not in the immediate vicinity of Jerry and the inmate. But they did hear him tell the inmate to strip and order him to do ten jumping jacks. They heard Jerry count as the inmate did the jumping jacks, and they heard him tell him to get dressed.

They all stated that they were in shock and disbelief when the incident happened, but it happened so fast that they couldn't stop it. They all knew that what they had just watched was really bad. One of them even asked the sergeant on duty if he could go home and open Christmas presents before coming back to do his report on the incident because he knew how bad this one was. One of them told the sergeant as they met at the top of the stairs, "I didn't do it," and pointed at Jerry.

The sergeant asked Corrections Deputy Jerry what he had done. He stated that he had made the inmate do jumping jacks and that "nothing fell out of his ass." The sergeant told him to fill out a strip search form even though what he had done was not considered a proper strip search under our policies.

When the field training officer (FTO) expressed his frustration about what the Corrections Deputy Jerry had done, the sergeant said he should have stopped him. She told the FTO that it was everyone's responsibility to stop bad behavior even though it is hard and uncomfortable to do so. She explained to the FTO that Jerry had a history of this type of activity. "In the past, he was known for this type of behavior, and it was looked upon as funny, but today this type of behavior is not tolerated."

It needs to be fully understood that this corrections deputy had done things like this for the past twenty years, had a reputation for being a clown, and had gotten away with it. The reason this incident took place can be summed up by what the sergeant told Jerry concerning his behavior. A transcript of the internal investigation stated that "…this conduct will not be tolerated…the administration of Sheriff Knezovich has a high standard of professionalism… What corrections deputies used to get away with before Sheriff Knezovich took office is not what corrections deputies get away with now…The behaviors we used to do are not acceptable behaviors now. This administration will not tolerate such behavior because we are to be professional at all times."

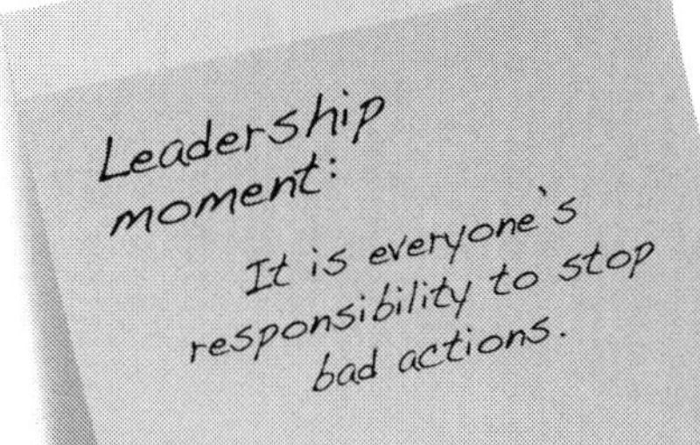

It is everyone's responsibility to stop bad actions.

Any of this resonating with leaders and would-be leaders reading this book? It is everyone's responsibility to stop bad actions the moment they are known. The other corrections deputies on the floor did not stop this action from happening. Everyone knew that the offending corrections deputy was a "clown" and had done similar things for twenty years. As leaders, we should never hear, "We saw it coming." Everyone in the jail I talked to, who had worked with Corrections Deputy Jerry, made this infamous statement: They all saw it coming.

My reply? "If you saw it coming, why didn't you do something to stop it?" The reason is summed up in three words: lack of leadership.

In chapter two, we talked about a leader's responsibility to uphold standards. When leadership fails to address bad behavior, the result is this kind of reprehensible act.

During the arbitration hearing concerning this incident, a thirty-five-year supervisor of the Sheriff's Office stated that Jerry was a "self-admitted jailhouse clown" who maybe should have been disciplined for his past actions toward inmates. Ask yourself, if you were in charge of the jail, how would you respond to this type of activity taking place under your watch. Uphold your agency's standards and you'll never have to answer this question.

How did we know he did this as a joke? Simple. He said so. He told the internal affairs investigator that he "had directed the inmate to do the jumping jacks for the inmate's safety as a 'self-initiated strip search.'" When asked what outcome he was looking for, Corrections Deputy Jerry stated, "To make sure he didn't have anything shoved up his butt or under his arms or anything like that. And to me it was just a gag that…I shouldn't have done."

When asked if making the inmate do jumping jacks was meant to be a strip search to find missing blanket parts or if it was a joke, he stated that it was both. He then clarified his answer: "It was more of a joke kind of thing."

He also told the investigator that his sergeant had told him that jail personnel "can't do those kinds of things anymore." He went on. "We used to, you know, play the games, have fun and everything else, but we can't do those things anymore."

> "I know this [directing inmates to do jumping jacks, but not strip naked] has been allowed before and this was accepted and witnessed in the past by the majority of the Jail Supervisors… but we just can't do the things we used to do in the past."

Once again, it is imperative to set, uphold, and enforce the standards of your organization.

To our would-be leaders, what do you think? Do you see any issues with this scenario? Think about this. Jerry's next statements will hopefully help you understand why high standards within in your organizations are so important. They aren't a joke.

In a letter to me, Jerry reiterated what he told the investigator about getting away with this kind of behavior in the past.

Then, during his disciplinary hearing, Jerry told me, "I was wrong. I admit I'm wrong, and... I can assure you it would never happen again." He again stated that he had previously "directed inmates to do jumping jack...at the time to be funny," and he said, "I never really thought about it before...You know, I was kind of the...the jail clown."

Further, during the arbitration hearing he stated, "I ordered an inmate to do jumping jacks in the jail intake area, in the presence of sergeants and lieutenants, just to be funny. This incident occurred before my 2005 assignment to a task force."

Small breaches of policy or procedures, when ignored, lead to major breaches which can turn into violations of the law and people's civil rights.

This incident is a classic example of what happens when an agency permits bad actions and does not uphold standards at any level. These are the types of incidents that led to the public trust crisis we see in law enforcement today. Let little breaches of policy or procedure slip, and you will see not only major breaches of policy and procedure, but violations of the law and people's civil rights.

Leadership moment:
Small breaches of policy or procedures, when ignored, lead to major breaches which can turn into violations of the law and people's civil rights.

Everyone saw it coming. And nobody did anything to stop it. Leadership failed this deputy, the entire corrections staff, the Sheriff's Office as a whole, and our community because they did not teach staff and supervisors to uphold standards. Supervisors did not want to be the bad guys or make people feel bad. They wanted to be liked. Leadership also tried to avoid making the union angry and looked the other way all those years. The cost of this type of failure is immeasurable when it comes to the amount of public trust lost.

Again, based on the fact pattern of the incident and the resulting investigation, Corrections Deputy Jerry was terminated. Anyone that is willing to abuse a mentally ill, suicidal inmate definitely doesn't deserve to wear a badge.

But despite all of this, he got his job back.

Arbitration Decision #2

The arbitration hearing concerning this incident was unique, let's say. During the hearing, the union attorney pulled me aside when we were on break.

Attorney: Sheriff, you can see we really aren't going to fight you too hard on this one.

Me: I really don't understand why you are fighting me at all on this one.

Attorney: Well, the corrections deputy is very well liked, and, if it had been anyone else, we wouldn't have fought you at all.

Me: Let me get this straight. You're fighting because the union and jail staff like him, but if they didn't like him, they wouldn't fight for him. Really?

Attorney: That's it.

Me: Remind me never to be part of your union. Unions are supposed to defend you if you are being unjustly treated, not because they like you or don't like you.

This case and the subsequent actions of unions during my efforts to change state law resulted in my complete loss of faith in unions.

However, this story isn't over. It only gets better. During the hearing, my attorney informed me that he may have made a mistake in agreeing to this arbitrator. He told me that this arbitrator has a history of ruling in the union's favor on cases like this. Really????

And it keeps getting better. When we came back from the break, during which the union attorney had told me, "We're not fighting you too hard on this one," the arbitrator stopped the hearing and suggested that both sides get together and come to a settlement on this.

What?

Arbitrator: I recommend both parties meet and come to an agreed settlement.

Me: Are you telling me that I have to settle this?

Arbitrator: I'm strongly recommending that both parties come to a settlement on this.

Me: Are you ordering me to come to a settlement on this?

Arbitrator: I'm ordering you to meet and come to a settlement on this.

All I could think was, "How in the world do you settle something like this? How do you get a fair settlement when the other side knows that if they don't settle, the worst they are going to see is the arbitrator giving their job back with some back pay?"

And that is exactly what happened. Corrections Deputy Jerry knew he was holding all the cards and would not come to a reasonable settlement, so the case went back to the arbitrator.

In his own words, the Arbitrator stated

(note: Grievant refers to Corrections Deputy Jerry):

- I find that Grievant's direction to Inmate X to do naked jumping jacks was not primarily motivated by safety concerns but instead was based largely on Grievant's personal whim. Grievant directed Inmate X, as a joke or gag, to strip and do jumping jacks. The County proved Grievant engaged in misconduct.
- During Sheriff Knezovich's administration, the County discharged three employees who engaged in misconduct similar in severity to Grievant's misconduct.
- In the incident involving Grievant, the County disciplined the sergeant for her response to the Greivant's actions; the County therefore did not ignore the shortcomings of personnel other than Grievant.
- The County faced potential civil rights and other legal claims over Grievant's misconduct.
- While Grievant was a 20-year employee with no disciplinary record, that factor has minimal significance in evaluating just cause discipline for this case of serious misconduct.
- During the investigation, Grievant admitted that his actions were wrong and assured the County that he would no longer engage in that misconduct. He has learned that his misconduct was wrong, and it is highly unlikely that he will repeat that misconduct.
- Grievant clearly engaged in reprehensible misconduct which, standing alone, could warrant discharge. However, two significant mitigating factors apply:
  a) Before 2005, Grievant had a history of acting like "the jailhouse clown" and was not previously disciplined for his clown like actions.
  b) The County did not disprove or counter Grievant's testimony that, during a prior Sheriff's administration, Grievant had directed a clothed inmate to do jumping jacks.
  c) Grievant referred to himself as "the jail clown."
  d) The sergeant stated during the investigation that the Grievant "in the past, was known for this type behavior and it was looked upon as funny, but today, this type of behavior would not be tolerated," and she testified that Grievant has "always been a practical joker."
  e) A 35-year employee of the Sheriff's Office established that Grievant was a "self-admitted jailhouse clown" and that perhaps Grievant should have been disciplined for his past acts toward inmates in that role.
  f) Employees who witnessed the event did not make any effort to stop Grievant.

     One possible explanation for their failure to stop him is that they were somehow under the clearly wrong understanding that such conduct by Grievant was somehow permitted in the workplace culture, consistent with Grievant's "jailhouse clown" reputation.

     A second possible explanation for their inaction is that Grievant's direction to Inmate X may have been so out of the ordinary that it shocked or startled the FTO and other corrections deputies into inaction.
  g) third explanation for their inaction is that Grievant had significantly more seniority than the FTO and the other corrections deputies, but that factor obviously should not have stopped them from stopping him.
  h) The fact remains: nobody stopped Grievant.

So, what was his ruling?

- Grievant's responsibility for his reprehensible misconduct is colored by those two factors.
- Due to that context, Grievant's actions in the incident with Inmate X do not rise to the level of such an extremely serious offense as to warrant summary discharge.
- The principles of just cause call for progressive discipline.
- With full consideration of all of the above, I conclude that the County's summary discharge of Grievant violated the parties' agreement that discipline would be imposed for just cause.
- I conclude that the discipline the County could have imposed on Grievant for just cause, as of the date of the conclusion of the investigation, ranged up to a 30-day suspension.
- The County fired Grievant on March 29, 2011. The processing and arbitration of the Union's grievance took 14 months.
- Reinstatement without back pay for that entire 14-month period would be an excessive sanction.
- All things considered I set aside the discharge and order the County to reinstate Grievant, impose a 30-day suspension on Grievant, and make Grievant whole.
- The make whole remedy requires that Grievant's back pay be offset by the amount of any income he received from interim employment.

So now we see what happens when leadership does not uphold its standards. The corrections deputy got his job back (with back pay) because:

1. Everybody knew about his behavior and nobody stopped him, even though they saw it coming.
2. Jerry was the "the jailhouse clown" who had not been previously disciplined for his clown-like actions. Leadership did not uphold, teach others to uphold, or enforce their standards. He got away with this sort of behavior his entire career. As a result, his actions became the culture of the agency.

Regardless of the prior administration's lack of leadership, none of the above logic justifies the arbitrator giving Jerry his job back. This should not have happened. He should not have been given his job back because his actions were reprehensible and, in the arbitrator's own words, caused the Sheriff's Office to face "potential civil rights and other legal claims over Grievant's misconduct." I'll never understand how the arbitrator overcame this fact.

Once the internal investigation was over, I gave the entire disciplinary packet to the U.S. Attorney for Eastern Washington to review for criminal civil rights violations.

What happened next was the last straw. I lost faith in the entire system.

When the U.S. Attorney was done reviewing the packet, we had the following discussion:

U.S. Attorney: Ozzie, if you hadn't handled it the way you did, we would have been all over you. However, since you handled it right and you terminated him, we're going to deactivate the file.

Me: What do you mean deactivate the file?

U.S. Attorney: You handled it, so we're not going to pursue charges.

Me: He could get his job back.

U.S. Attorney: You still handled it right.

Me: So, he gets away with abusing this inmate?

U.S. Attorney: He didn't get away with it. You terminated him.

Me: So that's it.

U.S. Attorney: Yes.

Really???

Did you catch it?

"Ozzie, if you hadn't handled it the way you did, we would have been all over you."

Me: Been all over ME.

Leadership moment:
Failure to train and failure to supervise are two of the leading reasons we get sued. Failure to supervise and failure to stop bad actions can get you prison time.

Failure to train and failure to supervise are two of the leading reasons we get sued. Failure to supervise and failure to stop bad actions can get you prison time.

Yes, future leaders, they will be all over you. We get sued for failure to train and failure to supervise. We can go to prison because we fail to supervise and fail to stop bad actions. If you don't believe me, I refer you to the case of Rodney King. We saw supervisors go to prison for what happened there.

Folks, leaders must lead. They must set the example and uphold standards. Regardless of outcomes such as this arbitration decision, we have to hold the line. You have to realize that even when you do all the right things, you can still end up with a problem employee getting his job back. Decisions such as this will continue as long as the arbitration system ignores the facts and merits of the case.

When a system devolves to the point of being more concerned about appeasing bad actors and their unions than doing what is right or wrong, something needs to change. Balance and the rule of law had to be restored to an extremely broken system. I decided to try and change the system. What followed entirely destroyed my faith in not only unions, but our state's legislative system.

After Jerry's arbitration decision, I contacted the executive director of my association, the Washington Association of Sheriffs and Police Chiefs (WASPC). He agreed that it was a bad arbitration decision and that we needed to do something. He stated that WASPC would be behind me on this one.

Little did I know what "behind you" would really mean.

Chapter 5
Selling Out Integrity
Have you forgotten who runs the State of Washington? The Unions.

As we dive into chapter five, it is important to distinguish several groups from one another. Government loves acronyms, and so many of these acronyms sound the same. It can get confusing. For the purposes of this book, there are two unions that played a major role in the story.

These unions are:

- DSA – Spokane County Deputy Sheriff's Association: This is the union of my deputies, serving deputies in the Spokane County Sheriff's Office from the rank of deputy through sergeant.
- WACOPS – Washington Council of Police and Sheriffs: This is one of four state-wide unions that serve a variety of locations and agencies. The DSA is a member of WACOPS.

There is another group that came into play.

- WASPC – Washington Association of Sheriffs and Police Chiefs: This is NOT a union, but rather an association representing police chiefs and sheriffs in the State of Washington.

It is important to note that I was raised believing that the true heart of unions is to ensure workplace safety and livable wages. They also ensure that the rights of the employees are upheld during disciplinary issues. The sad part is many unions are no longer interested in making sure everybody is doing their job. Rather, they spend their time protecting the lowest common denominator, which leads to morale problems throughout agencies.

Back to the story.

When the arbitration decision involving Corrections Deputy Jerry came back, I reached out to a person I had grown to respect, Don Pierce. Don had been a police chief in the State of Washington and in the State of Idaho. He had seen his share of controversy and had handled it well. Our association, the Washington Association of Sheriffs and Police Chiefs (WASPC), had hired Don as our executive director. One of his responsibilities was to lobby the legislature on our behalf in an effort to pass legislation supported by the sheriffs and police chiefs throughout the state. If I was going to have any chance of changing the law, I knew I needed Don's help.

On November 10, 2011, I emailed Don a copy of the arbitration decision involving Deputy Dave, who had damaged the truck, and asked him to review it. It didn't take long for him to respond.

> On 10 Nov 2011, Don Pierce wrote:
> "Well, I read the whole thing. Incredible. We have a systematic problem. I have put the whole issue on the agenda for our next board meeting. How can we be held accountable when we don't have the tools to fire someone who breaks the law ON Duty no less."

Don and I had several phone conversations during the following months. I used the time to highlight the problem to the media, while Don made plans to bring this to the attention of the legislature. I met with the editorial board of our local newspaper, The Spokesman-Review, concerning this issue and the possibility of presenting legislation to correct it. The editorial board published an opinion piece on January 11, 2012, titled, "Editorial: Sheriff, chief need power to restore public trust." I sent Don a link.

Editorial: SHERIFF AND CHIEF NEED POWER TO RESTORE PUBLIC TRUST

January, 11, 2012

Imagine you're a private employer who cannot fire an employee because you're unable to point to policies that definitively state that workers should not commit crimes, or lie to their bosses. And even when you clearly establish cases of crimes and the mendacity, you are stymied because lenient arbitrators disagree with the level of punishment.

Welcome to the world of sheriffs and police chiefs in Washington, where upholding integrity, ethics, and the law is a perilous minefield. Law enforcement chiefs need the leeway to establish discipline and punish their workers, but labor laws, court rulings, union contracts, and arbitrators keep running interference.

The latest imbroglio involves a deputy sheriff who was fired by Spokane County Sheriff Ozzie Knezovich and reinstated by an arbitrator. Arbitration can be a cost-effective tool for dispute resolution, but, as this case shows, the system needs to be refined.

The arbitrator did not dispute Knezovich's case against Deputy Sheriff…but she ruled that the punishment didn't fit the wrongdoing. The violations included criminally slashing the upholstery of a car with a knife and ticketing a motorist nine times for one stop because she wasn't sufficiently respectful.

The irony just hangs there.

Law enforcement officers want respect, but they battle for special consideration when they step over the line. Then their lawyers take over, asking for the whereabouts, in writing, of standard grade-school expectations, such as abiding by the law and telling the truth.

We have seen how difficult this has made it for Knezovich and former Spokane Police Chief Anne Kirkpatrick to restore public trust after a series of infamous cases involving law enforcement. A 2009 state Supreme Court ruling hasn't helped. In that case, a West Side officer who had clearly lied and ignored orders was reinstated, in part because it couldn't be clearly established that telling the truth was an essential function of the job.

The mind boggles.

In reaction to all of this, Knezovich says he will soon distribute a memo telling deputies they will lose their jobs for lying, drunken driving, or committing other crimes while on duty. He shakes his head that such obvious items must be put in writing. He expects union push-back.

The Sheriff also notes that the Washington Association of Sheriffs and Police Chiefs is discussing the possibility of a bill that would limit arbitrator discretion. Under the change, arbitrators could only overturn employee dismissals if they disagreed with factual findings. If there was agreement, as there was in the Deputy…case, the punishment would stand.

This and other reforms are warranted to reverse the decline in respect for law enforcement, which is too often self-inflicted.

By this time, Don was in full swing trying to build a coalition within the state legislature and was steadily making contacts to gain support for a new bill. When the editorial was published, he emailed Washington State Legislators Rep. Christopher Hurst, Sen. Adam Kline, Rep. Mike Hope, Rep. Brad Klippert, Sen. Jerome Delvin, and Sen. Mike Padden a message with the editorial included.

This is an excerpt of the exchanges that took place from that email, which is a part of the public record.

On Jan 2012, Don Pierce wrote:

"Please take a look at the editorial from the Spokesman.

"We are strongly considering trying to do something this session or next. We see this as the most important thing the Legislature can do in the area of public trust in law enforcement. Being forced to retain officers who have been determined to lie or commit crimes must end. We have no problem with the current due process rights for officers. However, if they are found to have committed the offense, punishment should not be altered."

Don Pierce, WASPC

On Jan 2012, Senator Devlin responded:

"It ought to be for all public employees who steal public monies and lie to employers by limiting the arbitrator's discretion."

On Jan 2012, Senator Kline responded:

"Didn't we deal with this issue a few years ago? Do I recall a sheriff or chief (Kitsap? Pierce?) fired an officer for lying about some activity, the cop lawyered-up with the help of the Teamsters and went to arbitration, and the arbitrator went the cop's way because there's nowhere in the manual it says you can't lie. This is Deja vu all over again."

As we covered in chapter two, Senator Kline was right. WASPC had attempted to pass this legislation before in 2010.

On Jan 2012, Don Pierce responded:

"You are close. The State Supreme Court ruled in a Kitsap County Deputy firing that the state did not have stated public policy that officers should tell the truth. We introduced legislation much as described in the editorial, but the police unions killed it, and we settled for a simple statement that the state had a public policy interest in honest cops. The real problem has not been solved. Arbitrators just hate to let a termination stand. I understand their empathy, BUT there is a strong public interest in holding police officers MORE accountable than we would other occupations. Sooner or later we have to quit putting a bandaid on this. It is not so much the ones that get overturned as the higher number that never get fired because the HR Department and attorneys advise that the officer will win given the past history of the arbitration decisions. Here is the language we proposed before:

'In the event that any person holding an office, place, position or employment under the provisions of this chapter has been found by the appointing authority by a preponderance of the evidence to have engaged in an act or acts of dishonesty or untruthfulness in the discharge of his or her official duties and has been terminated or otherwise disciplined by his or her employing agency; unless an arbitrator overturns the findings of dishonesty or untruthfulness, the arbitrator shall not substitute his or her judgment for that of the appointing authority and shall not overturn or otherwise overrule the termination or disciplinary action.'

We would now add 'engaged in illegal behavior, used excessive force…'"

On 20 Jan 2012, Don Pierce wrote:

Sheriff,

Attached is the bill draft. That is the good news. The bad news is that Senator Kline does not want to hear this bill this year. His committee is already jammed and we are almost at cut off (short session). We did have a great meeting though. He has agreed to sponsor the bill next year and move it. He also told us to meet with unions (WACOPS and Fraternal Order of Police) and tell them he wants this so get on board with WASPC. This gives us time to drum up support and get co-sponsors. This is probably good in the long run. Mitch was at the meeting and concurs with this strategy.

Don Pierce, WASPC

While Don continued to work on building a coalition between WASPC and the legislature, along with trying to work with the unions (WACOPS and Fraternal Order of Police), I worked on building a coalition of state representatives and senators associated with the Spokane County region and the police chiefs within the local jurisdictions of Spokane County.

Everywhere I went, I tried to get our legislators to commit to coming on board. You would think that this would have been an easy task since twelve of the fifteen state legislators associated with Spokane County were Republican.

Wait, before you start with the "oh, here we go, only Republicans care about holding people accountable" line, let's make it clear right now that is not what I'm saying. There is a simple reality in U.S. politics. Democrats are more sympathetic to unions than Republicans.

Stupid in my opinion, but the reality all the same. It will be an interesting dynamic in the American political structure the day Republicans find a way to work with unions.

I assume many of you are going, "Hey, I thought you weren't making this an R vs. D thing here, Sheriff." I'm not. I'm simply stating fact.

I am a Republican who grew up a Democrat. I even ran for office in Wyoming as a Democrat. Wyoming Democrats are some of the most conservative people I've ever met; they make Spokane Republicans look like progressive liberals. What made us Democrats? Labor issues.

The area I grew up in was a coal mining area. The United Mine Workers of America union influence was heavy. Their past president, John L. Lewis, was near deity in the eyes of the old timers. So, this is why I truly believe that the day the Republican Party stops demonizing unions and learns to work with them on issues is the day the Democrats need to start worrying.

I worked to build a bipartisan coalition with Spokane County legislators from both parties to support the bill. In April 2012, while attending a worker's memorial event, I tried to get Third Legislative Representative Timm Ormsby to chat with me about the bill. Timm is also the leader of the local labor coalition. I could tell something was up because he was doing everything he could to avoid me, something that was unusual. I had always had a good relationship with him, but it seemed this issue was something he did not want to discuss.

I would find out just how much he did not want to discuss it that December, when I presented the bill as one of my goals at a luncheon put on by the League of Women Voters. As I finished speaking about the bill, I could tell Timm was not pleased, especially when I heard him mumble, "We'll see about that." This kind of caught me off guard.

Coalition building was the order of the day in 2012, but it wasn't going well. By the end of 2012, only five of the fifteen legislators who represented districts within Spokane County agreed to sign on or sponsor the bill. Senators Mike Padden and Michael Baumgartener, out of the fourth and sixth legislative districts, agreed to co-sponsor the legislation in the Senate. Senator Padden was the chair of the Senate's law and justice committee. Representatives Kevin Parker, Joel Kretz, and Susan Fagen agreed to support the bill, with Representative Parker sponsoring the bill in the House.

I thought I could get Rep. Marcus Riccilli to sponsor the bill, even though he is a Democrat. Marcus is a good man, and we had what I thought was a strong friendship. Sadly, party dogma, union support, and jealousy led to statements like, "If Parker gets the majority of the credit, I'm out," and, "Ozzie, Lisa taught me not to waste political capital if the votes aren't there, and I'm telling you the votes aren't there."

So, coalition building was not going well. Remember when Senator Kline told Don he would help, but not in 2012? Well, by September of 2012, it was WASPC saying, "This needs to be done, just not in 2013."

What???

By our fall quarterly meeting in 2012, WASPC did a 180-degree about-face on the issue. I was on the WASPC Executive Board and held the position of president-elect, meaning that in May of 2013, I would be the president of WASPC. So, perhaps you can understand my extreme feeling of betrayal when, at our fall quarterly meeting in Leavenworth, Washington, Don told me that WASPC would not be supporting the Law Enforcement Integrity First Bill in 2013.

I think he could see the disillusionment in my face and quickly began to explain how WASPC had to support the Director of the Washington Criminal Justice Training Commission, Sue Rahr, in getting more money for the Training Commission so they could put on more academy classes.

Some people have asked me, "Sheriff, why couldn't WASPC do both, support the Law Enforcement Integrity First Bill and fight for money for the Training Commission?"

It wasn't that simple, that's why. This is where politics came in and things got really complex. Sue had convinced Don that the Training Commission and WASPC would need the help of WACOPS, the main police union coalition in the state to get the additional funding. With WACOPS on their side, the Training Commission and WASPC could use the power of WACOPS lobbyists to pressure the legislature into giving the Training Commission more money. But since WACOPS didn't like the Integrity First Bill, WASPC could only support one. And it wasn't going to be the Integrity First Bill.

Power and money, folks, power and money.

I tried to explain to Don that the ball was too far down the field. He and I had spent the past nine months building coalitions, working to gain public support, and promoting the Law Enforcement Integrity First Bill. I pointed out that WASPC could do both—work on the money aspect and push the bill. I tried to convince him that WACOPS would support more money for the Training Commission because it was to their advantage to do so. Don told me very bluntly that WACOPS had made it clear that if WASPC supported the Law Enforcement Integrity First Bill, they would work to defeat it. And to make matters worse, they would step away from the effort to get funding for the Training Commission.

Again, I tried to point out that WASPC could carry the water on the Training Commission funding on our own. He disagreed. The best I got was a promise for the issue to be discussed at our fall conference in November. From September to November, I continued to promote the Law Enforcement Integrity First Bill in the media and speaking engagements. All along knowing I had a very serious dilemma forming. What would I do if WASPC really did back out?

November came very quickly, and soon I was at the 2012 WASPC fall conference. Don seemed more resolute than ever that WASPC had to join forces with WACOPS and the Training Commission to gain the funding for the academy. I had only one hope. Take the issue to the Sheriff's Association. If I could get all the sheriffs on board, I might have a chance of saving the alliance with WASPC concerning the Law Enforcement Integrity First Bill.

So that's what I did. What I didn't see coming was WASPC's and the Training Commission's next move.

To give some background on this issue, Sue Rahr is the former Sheriff of King County, Washington's most populated county. She was also a member of the coalition led by Spokane Police Department Chief Anne Kirkpatrick when we tried to pass basically the same bill in 2010 (mentioned in chapter two). You may also remember that the unions, led by WACOPS, had fought that effort. The fallout was that Chief Anne Kirkpatrick received a vote of no confidence by the Spokane Police Guild in April 2010, Sheriff Rahr chose not to run again in 2012, and Chelan County Sheriff Mike Harum (also on the coalition) lost his 2010 election due to WACOPS' attacks.

A vote of no confidence happens when a union's membership votes to publicly state that they have no confidence in the leadership of the police chief or sheriff. It is a tactic that unions train local union leaders in and is used as a way to get rid of a chief or sheriff the union does not like. These kinds of votes can be a career killer.

This should give you a vision of what my future would be as a result of my push for the 2013 version of the same law, this time called the Law Enforcement Integrity First Bill.

For all you current chiefs and sheriffs, and those of you who want to wear the title and take upon yourselves those leadership mantels, votes of no confidence do happen, and for the most part you should wear them as a badge of honor.

The one thing the public needs to remember about a vote of no confidence is that it is a tactic actually taught by unions to local union leaders. It is designed to ensure a chief or sheriff does not stray too far from the wishes of the unions.

For the most part, we can wear them as badges of honor. I say "for the most part" because there are chiefs and sheriffs who are truly deserving of those votes because they are bad leaders. Unions will use votes of no confidence (and threats of them) to keep you in line. Let's face it, who wants to face the possibility of having the men and women you lead publicly say they have no faith in your leadership?

This is why such votes are so crushing to both the psyche and career of those who receive them. I watched what it did to my dear friend, Anne Kirkpatrick. I watched as it damaged her professional career for the next seven years. I am so proud of Anne because, even though this was the worst time of her life, she did not give up. I am even prouder that she was able to rebuild her career and that she is once again a police chief, this time of a major city police department.

During our fall WASPC meeting in November of 2012, the Sheriffs' Association held one of our quarterly meetings. To remind you, WASPC is a combined association consisting of sheriffs and police chiefs in Washington State. Sheriffs also have our own association. It was at this meeting that I presented the Law Enforcement Integrity First Bill to my fellow sheriffs and asked them to support my effort in getting this bill passed. This is when one of the most remarkable things happened. Don asked if Director Rahr could address our group. Of course, our former peer would be allowed to speak.

What Rahr had to say to the sheriffs, her former peers, said it all.

Rahr explained that the Training Commission was in need of more funding and that in order to get the funding, we needed WACOPS' help.

She went on to state that we were "throwing the baby out with the bathwater" in regard to the Law Enforcement Integrity First Bill. She finished by asking, "Have you all forgotten who runs the State of Washington? The unions do."

Leadership moment:

For all you current chiefs and sheriffs, and those of you who want to wear the title and take upon yourselves those leadership mantels, votes of no confidence do happen, and for the most part you should wear them as a badge of honor.

That was all it took. I watched the facial expressions of over twenty sheriffs, scanning for signs that Rahr's words were having the desired effect. What I saw was frankly heartwarming. As soon as she stated that the unions ran the State of Washington, I watched every one of those sheriffs clench their jaws.

Almost immediately, one of the most respected sheriffs of the group, Sheriff Bill Elfo, offered a motion, "I make a motion to support Ozzie's bill." There was an immediate second and a unanimous vote yes. Both Don and Rahr were rocked by the suddenness of the motion and the vote. I could tell that both were furious.

After the meeting, Don walked up to me and told me that since I had such great influence over the sheriffs, he'd see how well I would do with the legislature, making it very clear that WASPC would be sitting this one out. The sheriffs and I would stand alone. Thank goodness for the motto that sheriffs in Washington live by, "No Sheriff stands alone."

By mid-January of 2013, I had signatures from all thirty-eight of my peers supporting the Law Enforcement Integrity First Bill.

The sad fact would be that Rahr was right. The unions do run the State of Washington.

Why?

Well, as one State Representative told his Sheriff, "You don't write large checks at election time. The unions do." Once more, power and money would trump character and integrity.

In November of 2012, I was approached by the president of WACOPS, who happened to be a City of Spokane police officer.

WACOPS President: "Sheriff, what do you want to get out of this bill?"

Me: "I don't think a police officer should lie or commit crimes on duty. That's what I want to get out of this bill."

WACOPS President: "Can we negotiate the terms?"

Me: "I would be happy to."

At this point, he turned to his newly-appointed chief, Frank Straub, and stated, "See Chief, I can even negotiate with the Sheriff." Frank would go on to be the next casualty of the Spokane police unions.

Sounds promising, right? The unions are willing to negotiate. The WACOPS president and I had worked together successfully in the past, so I found those words promising. Sad thing is, I shouldn't have. Those negotiation meetings never happened. I tried and tried to reach out with no success. One of my deputies was on the WACOPS board, and I even reached out to him in order to get the meeting set. Soon it was January 2013, and the legislature was in session.

Representative Kevin Parker called a meeting between the sheriffs and WACOPS at his office in Olympia because of the failure on the part of WACOPS to set a meeting with me. Rep. Parker is a very good-hearted man and really wanted to help forge an agreement that all parties could support and bring this issue to resolution. On my way to Olympia for that meeting, I was feeling very hopeful and sure that the meeting would be a success. The WACOPS President and I both respected Rep. Parker. I had told Rep. Parker that WACOPS was willing to negotiate this issue. What could go wrong?

What indeed?

Chapter 6

The Threat, The Set Up, and The Trap

Sheriff, you've really pissed us off. If you don't back down now, we're coming after you.

By the time the date for the meeting with Representative Parker arrived, I had reached out to the WACOPS president using every avenue I could, with no success. Despite the fact that I knew he was dodging me, I still had great hope that the sit down would result in a good outcome. We had worked successfully on many issues together, and he had always been supportive of me.

I arrived in Olympia early and went to Rep. Parker's office. He had invited another representative to sit in on the meeting, along with a House legal advisor, a recorder, and WACOPS representatives. I had asked Sheriff Casey Salisbury to attend the meeting with me. It was a small meeting room. On one side of the room sat the WACOPS team, consisting of the president, a member of their executive board, and their lobbyist. The support staff were positioned in the background. As we were waiting for Sheriff Salisbury to arrive, Rep. Parker began the meeting by laying some ground rules and framing the question. Rep. Parker is a very nice person, intelligent and soft spoken. When he finished setting the stage, he asked the WACOPS team if they had any opening remarks. To say they did would be a slight understatement.

The Threat

The WACOPS lobbyist immediately zeroed in on me and began to speak just as Sheriff Salisbury was entering the room. He leaned forward, looking me right in the eye, and said, "Sheriff, you've really pissed us off. If you don't back down now, we're coming after you."

Sheriff Salisbury would tell you that I came out of my seat at this point, but that would be a little bit of an exaggeration. As soon as that lobbyist finished speaking, I leaned forward at the end of my chair, locked eyes with him, and told him very slowly, "You don't know me very well, do you? [Your president] should have told you that threats and intimidation don't work on me. If you want a piece of me, come and get it."

To say the rest of the folks in the room were stunned would be another understatement. Rep. Parker was shell-shocked; however, to his credit, he attempted to soften the exchange that had just taken place. He did a good job enforcing the ground rules he had established, and the discussion concerning the legislation began to take shape. As could have been predicted, WACOPS wanted to debate what constituted a lie. This is a classic union move, and if you remember, the Washington State Supreme Court had already removed the seriousness of lying.

It has always amazed me that when they get trapped in a lie, police officers—those who are trained to detect falsehoods and document them—seem to be the first to ask, "Well, is it really a lie? What is a lie anyway?"

Another favorite deflection tactic is to throw out the old, "Does this mean we can't use a ruse when we are trying to break a drug ring?" Translated into common terms, the point they are trying to make is that if an officer is working undercover and trying to infiltrate a drug ring, they may have to tell the bad guys a lie in order for the bad guys to trust them. This is how silly this argument becomes. Of course, the answer is no! The legislation does not mean that our undercover officers have to tell drug lords, "Hey one quick thing, I'm a police officer, and I'm here to eventually arrest you." Nor does it mean that if you are trying to find out just what a suspect knows that you can't give them some false leads in order to see if they really know the true facts of the case.

During this discussion, Sheriff Salisbury made one of the truest statements I've ever heard. "You know, if we were to ask a class of kindergarteners what a lie is, I bet they could tell us." So true, and yet so sad, that a child could tell you what a lie is, but grown adults, law enforcement officers no less, attempt to play games with such a simple concept.

After two hours of discussion, it was finally agreed that WACOPS would work on crafting an acceptable definition as to what constitutes a lie. Yes, we asked WACOPS to define a lie. We also asked them to bring to the table language they thought would be more acceptable to their rank and file concerning the entire bill, with one caveat: their language could not alter the intent of the legislation.

On January 24, Representative Parker published the following in his weekly legislative updates.

INTEGRITY FIRST

I have been working with Spokane County Sheriff Ozzie Knezovich on legislation which would not allow arbitrators to change the discipline decided by sheriffs and police chiefs when an officer has been found to have lied or broken the law. We're calling this legislation "Integrity First" because this is what we believe our law enforcement officers should be held to, integrity above all else.

Yesterday in my office I held a meeting with Sheriff Knezovich, Sheriff Salisbury from Mason County, the Washington Council of Police and Sheriffs President Craig Bulkley and representatives from all sides. Negotiations lasted nearly two hours, and we were able to make significant progress on a draft version of the legislation, which I plan to introduce on Friday. I am honored to have been a part of this process as we worked to: identify a problem, have discussions with stakeholders to find the best solution for all parties, and work together to move the proposal through the legislative process. I have heard from many of you already and I look forward to letting you know new developments in the coming weeks.

Little did Rep. Parker know that WACOPS had no intention of bargaining this issue in good faith and that the threat they made during our January 23 meeting was not just a shot across our bow. We also did not know the depth of their planning as to how this threat would be carried out.

The Set Up

For the next three weeks, Rep. Parker and I were in constant contact via phone and email trying to find a compromise position with WACOPS. Every time we thought we were close, WACOPS would throw another hurdle up. Some of this was because some of the other statewide police unions, like the Fraternal Order of Police, were being more militant than WACOPS, and out of fear of losing membership, WACOPS began developing an even harder line.

My respect for the president of WACOPS had disappeared during our meeting with Rep. Parker, not only because of the threat, but also because of his inability to honestly negotiate this issue. Rep. Parker expressed his extreme frustration with him and WACOPS because of their waffling whenever it appeared we had a potential agreement.

Parker also expressed concern because Sue Rahr was pressuring him to push the bill out until 2014. Yes, Sue Rahr, the Director of the Criminal Justice Training Commission and former Sheriff.

Remember, WASPC and Rahr got into bed with WACOPS to kill the Law Enforcement Integrity First Legislation in exchange for WACOPS support to get more money for the Training Commission. They sold integrity out for dollars.

During the negotiation process, I noticed some interesting dynamics starting to take place. Retired members of the WACOPS Executive Board began hitting me with some fairly personal attacks, as did their president, who sent out the following letter.

January 22, 2013

Dear members of the State Legislature,

On January 17, 2013, Spokane County Sheriff Ozzie Knezovich wrote you a letter asking you to support legislation that would remove an arbitrator's discretion in discipline cases involving law enforcement officers.

He hails this legislation as "vital to protect our citizens, law enforcement as a profession, and to restore the public's trust in law enforcement." We find this statement, and the media attack he has launched against law enforcement officers, highly offensive. Especially when coming from an elected official that should represent the law enforcement profession with respect and honor.

A police officer's primary duty is to enforce and uphold the law. He is called upon to exercise tact, restraint and good judgment and represents law and order to the public. No one dislikes a "bad cop" more than the other peace officers that depend on him to fulfill his duties and to cover their backs in life threatening situations. On the other hand, no one should be denied due process or a fair hearing. The constitution guarantees this for all criminal suspects and for the employees charged with protecting the public.

Sheriff and police departments have disciplinary procedures that are meant to be followed in order to insure fairness. These procedures provide consistency so that favoritism does not play a part in determining appropriate discipline and allow mitigating circumstances to be considered. Most law enforcement officers in Washington State are subject to binding arbitration. In arbitration, a neutral third party is chosen to hear both sides of the case, and then resolves it by rendering a specific decision or award. The decision of the arbitrator is final.

The Sheriff is asking you to bypass the disciplinary process and tie the hands of the arbitrator so that he, as an elected politician, can be the only judge. He would leave you to believe that there are not already policies in place to insure fairness in the proceedings. This is simply not true.

- In 2010, the legislature unanimously enacted Chapter Law 294, creating a policy of the state that all law enforcement personnel must comply with their oath of office and agency policies regarding the duty to be truthful and honest in the conduct of their official business.
- The Sheriff's proposed legislation states that if the appointing authority finds an officer to have committed illegal acts, he can terminate the officer and an arbitrator cannot overturn that decision. This eliminates the court of law from the process and makes no differential between being accused and being convicted of a crime. It is already policy that being convicted of a felony is grounds for termination of a law enforcement officer.

The Washington Council of Police & Sheriffs believes that integrity in law enforcement professionals is vital to holding the public's respect and trust. And we believe that law enforcement officers, like all citizens, have the right to a due and fair process. The current standards of arbitration provide this and we ask you to maintain them.

Thank you for your consideration. Please feel free to contact us with any questions or concerns.

Did you catch it? "The Sheriff is asking you to bypass the disciplinary process and tie the hands of the arbitrator so that he, as an elected politician, can be the only judge."

Really?

He goes on. "The Sheriff's proposed legislation states that if the appointing authority finds an officer to have committed illegal acts, he can terminate the officer and an arbitrator cannot overturn that decision. This eliminates the court of law from the process and makes no distinction between being accused and being convicted of a crime."

Really?

These statements were never in our legislation.

It gets worse. By the time WACOPS was finished, they totally destroyed their integrity and would become poster children for why such a law is necessary. But hey, the Washington State Supreme Court had already stated that lying was protected speech.

The Retired Spokane County Deputy Sheriff's Association posted the following on their website.

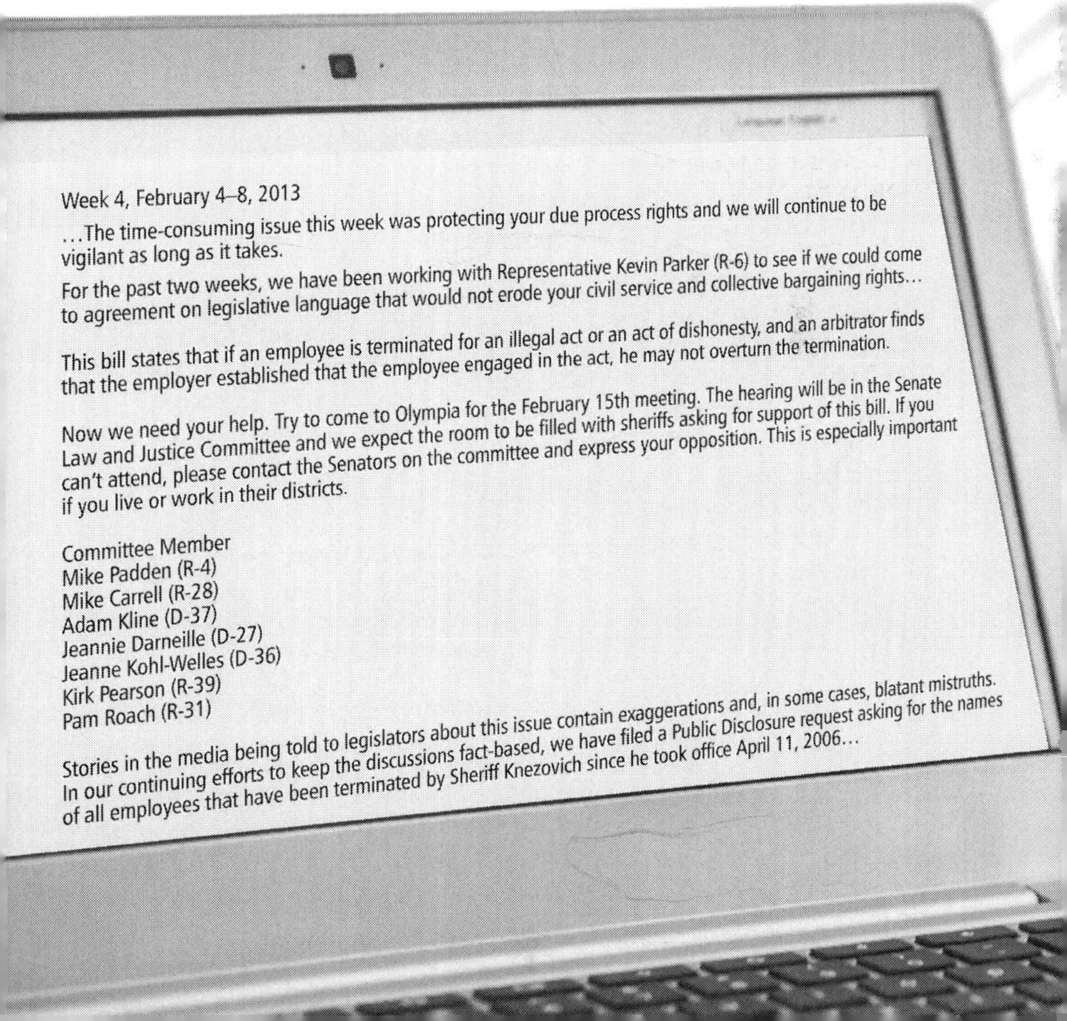

Week 4, February 4–8, 2013

...The time-consuming issue this week was protecting your due process rights and we will continue to be vigilant as long as it takes.

For the past two weeks, we have been working with Representative Kevin Parker (R-6) to see if we could come to agreement on legislative language that would not erode your civil service and collective bargaining rights...

This bill states that if an employee is terminated for an illegal act or an act of dishonesty, and an arbitrator finds that the employer established that the employee engaged in the act, he may not overturn the termination.

Now we need your help. Try to come to Olympia for the February 15th meeting. The hearing will be in the Senate Law and Justice Committee and we expect the room to be filled with sheriffs asking for support of this bill. If you can't attend, please contact the Senators on the committee and express your opposition. This is especially important if you live or work in their districts.

Committee Member
Mike Padden (R-4)
Mike Carrell (R-28)
Adam Kline (D-37)
Jeannie Darneille (D-27)
Jeanne Kohl-Welles (D-36)
Kirk Pearson (R-39)
Pam Roach (R-31)

Stories in the media being told to legislators about this issue contain exaggerations and, in some cases, blatant mistruths. In our continuing efforts to keep the discussions fact-based, we have filed a Public Disclosure request asking for the names of all employees that have been terminated by Sheriff Knezovich since he took office April 11, 2006...

Mistruths. Remember that word. It will become an overarching WACOPS strategy for the next two years. As can be seen above, WACOPS painted this as a total and utter erosion of their due process rights.

In addition, a retired Spokane County Sheriff's Office detective I had worked with sent a letter to the unions. He titled it, "Sheriff needs to be reigned in."

Below are some excerpts from my response letter, dated January 29, 2013.

> …This legislation does not overturn Due Process, Just Cause, or the arbitration process. The only change is, should the **Arbitrator** find that a Chief or a Sheriff has proven their case (by clear and convincing evidence), the **Arbitrator** in cases involving…**CRIMES** or **DISHONESTY**, cannot change the Sheriff or Chief's discipline.
>
> Your letter stated that an arbitrator would not be able to consider the following:
>
> - If the investigation was flawed or incomplete
> - If mitigating circumstances were considered
> - If portions of the bargaining agreement were violated
> - or any combination of the above factors.
>
> None of this is factual. As noted above, an **Arbitrator** would have to issue a **sustained finding** in the matter in order for the termination to stand. In order to have a sustained finding the arbitrator would have to find that:
>
> 1. The investigation was complete and factual
> 2. Mitigating circumstances had been weighed
> 3. There were no bargaining agreement violations
> 4. There was Just Cause to sustain the finding
>
> Mr. [redacted], as a former union president, you know this to be true…
>
> This legislation is not about affecting an arbitrator's ability to be a neutral, third party fact finder. The legislation specifically states that a Sheriff's or Chief's disciplinary decision stands **only** if the **Arbitrator** finds the Sheriff or Chief has proven their case.
>
> What this legislation is about is ensuring the integrity of the law enforcement profession and maintaining the public's trust by clearly stating law enforcement officers cannot commit crimes on duty or lie.
>
> Do you really disagree with this position?
>
> …You may find it informative to actually read the facts concerning these issues rather than forming your opinion based on one side of the issue and hearsay. I would be happy to review any and all of my disciplinary decisions with you.
>
> Sincerely,
> OZZIE D. KNEZOVICH, Sheriff
> Spokane County

In the letter, I also offered to meet with this retired detective to chat about this issue. He never took me up on it, which is kind of interesting. I considered him a friend. We spent countless hours together driving back and forth from Spokane to Olympia to attend WACOPS meetings when I was president of the Spokane County DSA.

When it comes to protecting bad cops—and that is exactly what WACOPS did in this case—friendships take a back seat. Hard lesson learned.

And so it went. I would write a letter to the legislature, and WACOPS or DSA would write a counter letter. This continued until February 15, 2013, the day that the Washington State Senate heard testimony from the opposing parties concerning the Law Enforcement Integrity First bill.

Fourth Legislative District Senator Mike Padden had scheduled the hearing, and since I was the lead for the pro side of this issue, I was to testify concerning the need for such legislation. If you recall, Senator Padden had agreed to sponsor the Law Enforcement Integrity First Legislation in the Senate. I knew Senator Padden well because the Fourth Legislative District is in Spokane County. The one thing that always troubled him about the bill was the fact that WASPC had not agreed to support it. Senator Padden told me several times that he felt that WASPC's lack of support weakened our effort. It made it look like our own association did not support the legislation, despite the fact that all thirty-nine Washington sheriffs had signed on to the legislation.

The Trap

On the morning of the hearing, I arrived at Senator Padden's Office early because he wanted to talk to me about how the hearing would go. He made it very clear that I would be at the hearing table for quite some time because his committee wanted to ask a lot of questions. He told me to be ready to recount the arbitration hearings which had led up to the crafting of the legislation. Senator Padden is a good person and was very concerned about this hearing since he was the Chair of the Senate Law and Justice Committee.

The time came for the hearing, and WACOPS and the rest of the unions went first. Scanning the room, I noticed one of my deputies, a WACOPS member and DSA executive board member. I found this odd since he would have had to receive clearance to take time off to attend the meeting, and that time off would have had to be approved by me. Lo and behold, my former friend, the retired detective, was also there, and he testified on behalf of WACOPS.

Several sheriffs had come in support of the bill and/or to testify in favor of the bill. Finally, it was my turn. I did something that day I don't normally do, and frankly it was the last time I did it. I read a prepared statement. Even though I thought the statement was good, reading one takes away two key aspects of effective communication, eye contact and the passion that comes from speaking from your heart.

Here, in its entirety, is what I said, or better put, read:

> Senators, thank you for conducting a hearing in reference to this proposed legislation. The question on everyone's mind is: what is this bill really about? The answer is the same that I gave the president of WACOPS and Spokane City Police Officer Craig Bulkley last November when he asked me that question. I and the other thirty-eight elected sheriffs of the State of Washington believe that we in law enforcement should not commit crimes on duty or lie. There is really nothing more to this bill than that.
>
> Contrary to information put out by WACOPS, this bill is not about doing away with arbitration, due process, just cause, or the disciplinary process. The bill specifically mentions the arbitrator's dominant role in the process.
>
> The Stage was set for this hearing when the Supreme Court ruled in a Kitsap County case that there was no strict standard of "explicit, well defined, and dominant public policy concerning a law enforcement officer being dishonest."
>
> This is the second time sheriffs and chiefs have come before you concerning this matter. In 2010, in response to the Supreme Court's ruling, the legislature passed RCW 43.101.021, which was a very watered-down version of the original SB6590 and weakly set policy that we should obey our oaths. The original bill's intent was that an arbitrator could not overturn a termination of a peace officer unless they also overturned the finding of dishonesty.
>
> Concerning Spokane County, in two cases arbitrators have sustained that the deputies committed crimes or civil rights violations on duty and then ruled to give their jobs back. Such acts damage the most vital bond between a peace officer and those they serve, which is the public's trust.
>
> You don't have to look far for examples of the damage these few peace officers have done. Seattle is under a DOJ review, Spokane's former mayor requested a DOJ review, the citizens of Spokane this week passed a resolution by sixty-nine percent of the vote to give a civilian Ombudsman power to independently investigate police conduct.
>
> This morning, history will mark the day the future of my profession's integrity was debated. History will record that the Washington State Senate heard testimony concerning legislation proposed by all thirty-nine elected sheriffs of the State of Washington stating that peace officers should not commit crimes on duty, nor should they be dishonest. To all the peace officers in this room, I ask, what are you going to say when one day your children ask what side of the line were you standing the day the integrity of law enforcement, of your profession, was debated in the halls of the Washington State Senate.

When I looked up, I noticed that Senator Padden had a look of near panic on his face. He quickly said, "Sheriff, thank you. You can go."

Go???? Remember, Senator Padden had prepared me all morning to sit

and field questions from his peers. I didn't hesitate and started to get up because I could see in his face that something was drastically wrong.

And then the trap slammed shut. As I was three-quarters of the way out of my seat, Washington State Senator Pam Roach suddenly said that she had a question for me. I saw Senator Padden turn pale. I sat down and acknowledged the Senator, and this is part of that exchange:

Senator Roach: "Would an example of a claim of dishonesty be a law enforcement officer pumping gas from a public pump for a private vehicle?"

Me: "Yes, it would. It would be a theft."

Senator Roach: "Have you ever done anything like that?"

Me: "No, I have not."

Senator Roach: "Never at all?"

Me: "Never."

Senator Roach: "Interesting. Thank you."

Sheriff, did she just call you a thief?

Why yes, she did. I couldn't believe what had just happened. Not only did she call me a thief, but she did it in the most public fashion possible. If you ever watch the tape of that hearing, and yes, you can still see it if you know where to look, you will also see how smugly and arrogantly she did it, especially when she pushed her mic away and said, "Interesting. Thank you."

Not many caught what had happened, but those who did were furious or gleeful, depending on which side of the issue they were on. The executive director for WASPC turned to the executive director for WACOPS and said that if this is the way they were going to play this, it wouldn't go well. WACOPS adamantly denied any knowledge that Roach was going pull this stunt. My deputy made a point of coming up to me and assuring me that he was not there to hear the testimony but was there instead in his capacity as a Criminal Justice Training Commissioner, and he kept pointing to the CJTC pin on his lapel. Senator Baumgartner was furious that Senator Roach would do this to me, especially since he had co-sponsored the bill.

I heard the retired detective claim something along the lines of, "I would have told him if I had known that this was going to happen." Needless to say, I was more in shock than angry at the time. I could tell that this had been a setup and that WACOPS, despite all of their denials, knew it was going to happen. That became clear once I had left the building and saw the WACOPS contingent huddled together around Representative Jeff Holy. Their glances in my direction and then towards the ground said it all. All this explained why there were so many people there that really should not have been at the hearing.

Before I left the building, I walked up to Senator Roach and asked her what was behind her question. She stated that she had been asked to question me. I explained to her that my political opponents during my first election had tried to claim I misused a gas card, when, in fact, I was authorized to use the gas card. She smugly replied, "Well, it looks like I was used." She wasn't used. She was a willing participant.

You may be wondering who put her up to it. Well, that "who" was State Representative Matt Shea, the most vocal opponent of the legislation out of any of our Spokane County Legislators, and an extreme political enemy.

How do I know that? Senator Roach told Senator Padden just before the hearing that she was going to ask a question for Rep. Shea. This is why Senator Padden tried to get me out of there. He knew what was coming.

The news of this spread like lightning. I got a call from Spokane County Commissioner Todd Mielke, asking what the hell had gone on. I told Todd that WACOPS had set me up and were trying to use the old gas card incident to destroy my credibility. Don't worry, I will explain that incident in the next chapter.

Leadership moment:
Understand that in today's political environment, if they can't beat you through logic, your opponents will often use false accusations to destroy your credibility.

But at that moment, I had a fire to deal with. They played their hand well. This falsehood was all it took.

There are politicians I know personally who have said things like, "We're going to put out false accusations in order to take our opponent off message and put them on defense. This should keep them off balance throughout the debate/campaign."

Understand that in today's political environment, if they can't beat you through logic, your opponents will often use false accusations to destroy your credibility.

Leaders, be prepared for it. If they can't beat you using logic and their own ideas or facts, your opponents will use false accusations and any other shady tactic they can to destroy your credibility.

I've had it happen to me multiple times. WACOPS did this and did this well throughout the entire debate on this issue right up until they themselves were used by the true forces behind this trap.

The next day, instead of the headline in the newspaper being about the debate, it was about the allegation of theft surrounding a political falsehood that was started seven years earlier.

Remember our discussion on how starting a false rumor can take your opponent off their message. Now you see how effective it is. I was now faced with trying to fight a two-front battle. I was faced with trying to fight for the Law Enforcement Integrity First Legislation on one front, mind you with a cloud over my head and with decreased credibility. The other front was the battle to defend my honor at the same time. Spread the lie, keep your opponent off message and off balance, drive your false message and agenda, and win. It worked for both WACOPS and Representative Shea in this battle.

They were able to defeat the legislation. Senator Padden could not even get the bill out of his own committee. The unions won the day.

Again, money trumped integrity.

The statewide Retired Deputy Sheriff Association posted this to their members:

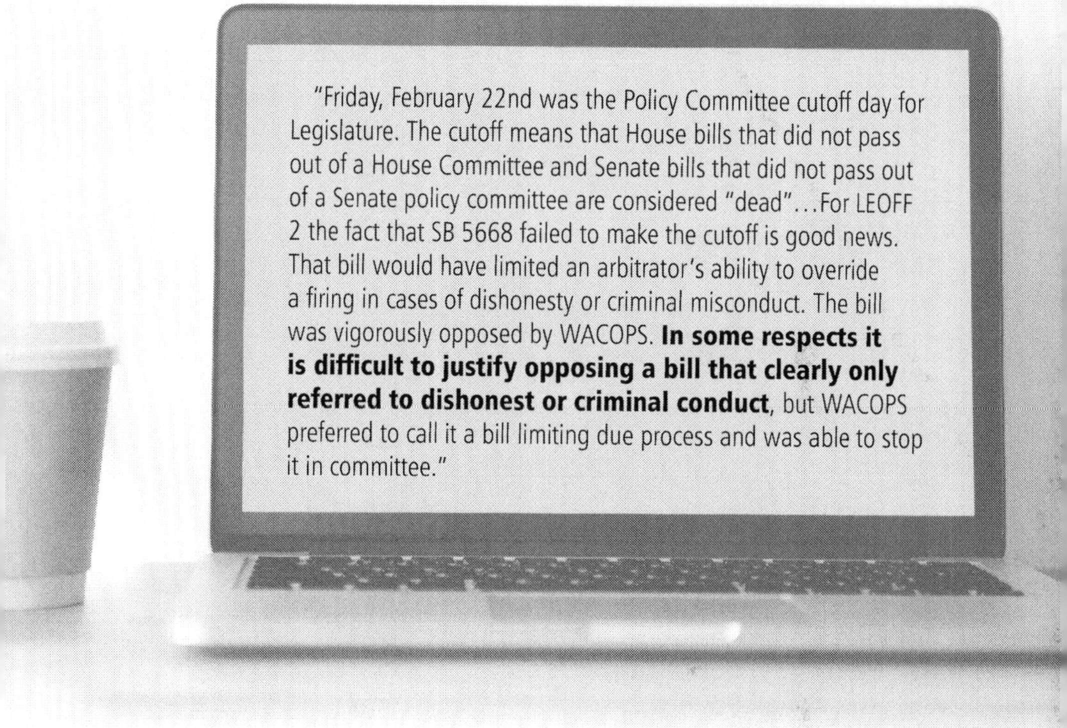

"Friday, February 22nd was the Policy Committee cutoff day for Legislature. The cutoff means that House bills that did not pass out of a House Committee and Senate bills that did not pass out of a Senate policy committee are considered "dead"...For LEOFF 2 the fact that SB 5668 failed to make the cutoff is good news. That bill would have limited an arbitrator's ability to override a firing in cases of dishonesty or criminal misconduct. The bill was vigorously opposed by WACOPS. **In some respects it is difficult to justify opposing a bill that clearly only referred to dishonest or criminal conduct**, but WACOPS preferred to call it a bill limiting due process and was able to stop it in committee."

Read it again, folks. "In some respects, it is difficult to justify opposing a bill that clearly only referred to dishonest or criminal conduct, but WACOPS preferred to call it a bill limiting due process and was able to stop it in committee."

Even the retired guys knew the truth about the Law Enforcement Integrity First Legislation, and even they had trouble justifying what WACOPS did. WACOPS effectively rebranded the intent of the legislation. Their strategy: lie and claim it is a bill limiting due process. It will die in committee.

WACOPS may have killed the legislation; however, in the long run, they really damaged themselves and would continue to damage themselves as they moved into the second phase of their plan, which you may recall was, "Sheriff, you've really pissed us off. If you don't back down now, we're coming after you."

And they did come after me. Their next move was designed to destroy me politically. However, they didn't count on a few things, one of which was my connections to people in the national media. WACOPS would soon find themselves on the national stage, and they would also find that they weren't the king, as they supposed. Rather, they were actually pawns in a much larger game.

WACOPS: Sheriff, I'm telling you, we didn't send that letter out. Check the postmark. We're in Olympia, and that letter was sent from Spokane.

Me: So, you are telling me someone stole your identity?

WACOPS: Uh, yes.

Chapter 7
WACOPS Stolen Identity
So, you're telling me someone stole your identity?

After their ambush at the Senate hearing, WACOPS and our local unions learned this fight would not be as easy as they thought. The citizens of Spokane County were not pleased, to say the least, when they read about Senator Roach's antics.

The outpouring of support was very welcome because I was still stinging from the Roach's innuendos. In order to put this falsehood to rest once and for all, I contacted the Spokane City Police Ombudsman and requested that he conduct an independent investigation into the allegations of gas theft.

The facts surrounding this incident are as follows:

On April 11, 2006, I was unanimously appointed Sheriff of Spokane County by the Spokane County Board of County Commissioners. The Commissioners knew that the Republican Party and the former Sheriff wanted the Sheriff's handpicked favorite. They appointed me instead. I soon found myself in a major dilemma: I was Sheriff and my entire command staff was made up of the former Sheriff's command team and my opponent's supporters. Even though I was appointed, I still had to run for office, and the primary was in four months.

Knowing I was truly the dark horse, I decided to ask some of the old command staff to stay on until after the election. I was concerned that if I replaced the old command staff and then lost the election, I would cause two more major upheavals, on top of the one that just happened as a result of my appointment as Sheriff.

I reasoned that if I replaced the current command staff, the new command staff would not have any job security if I lost the election. They would be seen as being traitors in the eyes of my opponent. So, I asked the old command staff to stay on until after the election.

The first person I asked to stay was our investigative captain, Bruce Mathews. Bruce is a good person and had been my boss once. He had actually stated once that he had to make sure I was ready to run the place someday. I'll never forget that comment. When he said it, all I could think was, "That will a be a cold day."

I explained my plan to Bruce, and what he said next was probably the soundest advice I have ever received, and frankly, one of those Nostradamus moments. You know the type. "Pay attention to what I'm telling you or you will regret it."

Bruce looked right at me and said, "Ozzie you need to replace every one of us as soon as possible. You need to form your own team around you, and you need to do that ASAP. I know you like to take care of people, but you need to listen and replace everyone now."

I was slightly taken aback. I knew Bruce had intended to retire when the new Sheriff came in, but I didn't quite know what to make of this. I did understand the warning within his words, and I should have listened. The old saying "keep your friends close and your enemies closer" is not always good advice. I know that everyone likes to point to the fact that President Lincoln appointed people to his cabinet who were political rivals, and it worked. I read that book too. But it doesn't always work.

Sometimes it is a bad idea to "keep your friends close and your enemies closer."

In order for Lincoln's concept to work, the people surrounding the leader must have the honor and integrity to put their own ambitions aside and work toward the greater good. For me, it was a mixed bag. One appointment to my command staff, Rick Van Leuven, was a supporter of my opponent. Ironically, he would become my closest friend and ally. The most important thing for a leader to do when selecting people for leadership positions is to make sure you are not selecting bobble heads or backstabbers. The moment you realize you have any of these on your command team, remove them. If you don't, it will cost you and your organization.

Leadership moment:
Sometimes it is a bad idea to "keep your friends close and your enemies closer."

Make sure you don't select bobble heads or backstabbers for your senior leadership team.

Instead of heeding Bruce's warning, I kept all but one of the old command staff. When I was appointed Sheriff, one of my undersheriffs came to me and said that he wouldn't do anything to hurt me, but he was still supporting my opponent. I should have had him define what he meant by, "I won't do anything to hurt you." It seemed that every time I turned around, I was putting out a fire only to find that this particular undersheriff was behind it.

One of the first things I was asked as Sheriff was if I was going to use my personal vehicle or a Sheriff's Office vehicle. Because I was in an election, and I did not want to risk being accused of using a Sheriff's Office vehicle to further my campaign, I chose to use my own vehicle. In doing so, I was entitled to a $560/month vehicle allowance. Because I was appointed and no one was sure I would win the primary in August, I was given a gas card to use instead of the monthly vehicle allowance. It didn't matter to me because I

Leadership moment:
Make sure you don't select bobble heads or backstabbers for your senior leadership team.

didn't plan on using the card much either.

So, to make things very clear, as part of my benefit package, I had a choice of a company car, a $560 per month vehicle allowance, or the use of a gas card when needed. At the time, I was driving a ¾-ton Dodge pickup that got about twelve miles to the gallon. Just driving back and forth from home to work was a forty-mile round trip, not to mention all the meetings I had to attend all over the county. The average price of gas in 2006 was $2.75/gallon. I used the gas card from April to June.

Simple math brings us to the fact that on a monthly basis, I was driving a minimum of eight hundred miles for work purposes.

800/12mpg X $2.75/gallon = $183.33 per month. $183.33 X 2.5 months = about $458.

In that two-and-a-half-month period, I should have charged the county a minimum of $458. In reality, I only charged $372. These numbers do not include any of the miles I drove throughout the county to attend meetings. They only reflect the minimum amount of mileage I drove my personal vehicle to work and back.

So, the $372 worth of gas I charged to the county gas card was far less than what I was entitled to if I had received the $560 per month vehicle allowance.

You may be thinking, "Okay Sheriff, so what's the big deal? You were entitled to use the gas card." Well, nothing is that simple in politics.

As I mentioned above, my primary election was in August 2006, and about two weeks before the ballots were to come out, the undersheriff who said he would do nothing to hurt me told me that an employee had brought it to his attention that I was using a county gas card. He said that he felt it was against county policy for me to do so.

What?? I didn't even bother to talk to him about it. I simply contacted the Spokane County CEO and asked him if I had violated county policy. He said that I had not violated county policy and that the county owed me mileage plus the cost of the gas.

I told him that I really didn't want to make an issue of this and that I had chosen the gas card option to avoid any accusations that I was using a county vehicle for my campaign. I know, go ahead and say it. I've said it to myself a hundred times since then. "How'd that work for you?"

I ended up right where I was hoping to avoid. I told the CEO that I

was going to pay the county back, to which he responded, "Why? You are entitled to the money and more."

I told him that there is no amount of money worth my integrity and that it just wasn't worth the fight.

You would think it would have ended there, right? Well, the undersheriff had been a very busy bee and had contacted the media. KXLY reporter Jeff Humphrey contacted me about the allegation, and I told him to talk to the County CEO. Jeff later let me know that he was not going to cover this story because there was nothing inappropriate about what had happened. Again, you would think that it would have ended there right.

Nope. The undersheriff and those who were not happy with my appointment or election have tried to bring this up in each and every one of my elections since, and I suspect they will continue to do so as long as I run for office.

So, now you know what all the fuss was about. My political opponents passed a falsehood onto Senator Roach, and she was more than willing to help them try to use it to destroy my credibility and reputation.

Writing that last sentence made me flash back to something my son asked me when the Roach allegation was going on. "Dad, why are they trying to destroy your character?" Hard to explain to a young man just how disgustingly evil the world of politics really is. It was harder seeing the pain in his eyes as he asked the question. Leaders, particularly elected leaders, must make sure their families are prepared for the negativity that comes with the top seat.

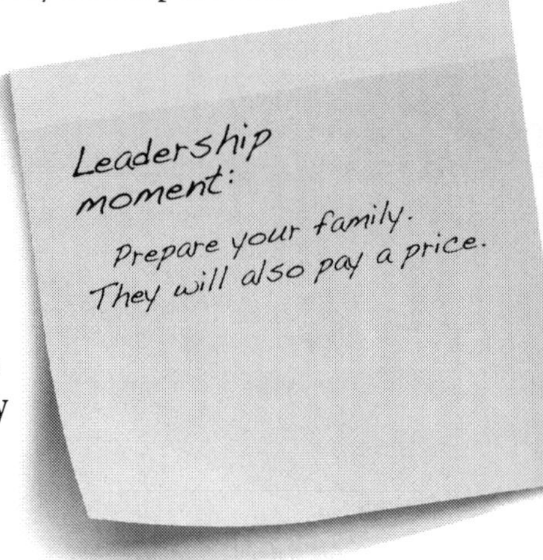

Prepare your family.
They will also pay a price.

For all the officers reading this, you know full well the price our families pay. They have to carry the full impact of all the negativity a police officer lives through, especially in today's environment. As a leader, that pressure is magnified a hundredfold. With that said, as a leader, it is your responsibility to help your deputies/officers and their families survive this constant pressure. Which at times means putting yourself between the media/activists and your deputies/officers.

Back to the Ombudsman. The Ombudsman's 2013 investigation came back exactly the same as every one of the prior investigations into this matter. I had broken no laws or policies and was actually entitled to far more money than I was actually given. Between the media, the county, and my own request for review, there were three investigations prior to the Ombudsman's involvement. But did the scrutiny end there? No. Since then, my opponents have always raised one flag concerning this investigation, the fact that the Ombudsman did not talk to the undersheriff.

Well, as fortune would have it, that former undersheriff stopped by the office one day. When I saw him, I grabbed my Internal Affairs (IA) sergeant and told him to set up an interview with the former undersheriff concerning this matter.

While talking to the IA sergeant, the former undersheriff hung himself. He had always maintained that an employee came to him with the information about the gas card. Problem is, that never happened. The IA sergeant asked who brought the gas card to his attention. He gave a name. He was then asked what he would say if we had documented proof that the employee he named had already stated she never brought the gas card to his attention. In fact, she had stated that she was the employee who told me to use the gas card. Needless to say, he has never been back to the Sheriff's Office.

As I was still dealing with the fallout of Senator Roach's false accusation, WACOPS wasted no time capitalizing on the perceived damage they had caused me as a result of Senator Roach's question. I received yet another letter from WACOPS. The following excerpts show how strongly they held to their lie about the bill.

February 18, 2013

Sheriff Knezovich,

I continue to share your belief that law enforcement officers should be held to the highest standard of integrity but we are still not convinced that there is a need for this legislation and do not want to rush into overturning 40 years of established labor law without adequate facts...

Testimony given February 15th in the Senate Law and Justice Committee reinforced our belief that a neutral party should be able to consider mitigating circumstances...

Because you have admitted, and there is clear and convincing evidence, that you put publicly funded gas into a private vehicle, you could have been terminated for that answer if you were an employee in a formal interview. Under current law, an arbitrator would consider the mitigating circumstances - that you were pre-approved for the practice and that you repaid the county - and that arbitrator would have had the option of reinstating your employment. This due process is what we are trying to protect.

...I think we all agree that the vast majority of officers serving at the state, city, and county level exercise tact, restraint, and good judgment. If there are criminals and liars wearing badges, we need to identify who they are and how they were able to retain their Commissions so we can work together for a solution. We don't believe SB 5668 is that answer...

I have also asked [the] Executive Director of WASPC, to provide us examples of arbitration decisions that were overturned when a law enforcement officer had committed a criminal act or an act of dishonesty, and, that all agreed upon disciplinary procedures had been followed. I have not received that information.

Really? Let's break the letter down.

"Because you have admitted, and there is clear and convincing evidence, that you put publicly funded gas into a private vehicle, you could have been terminated for that answer."

1. WACOPS' spin on Senator Roach's question was impressive. The statement does not even remotely reflect Senator Roach's question nor my answer.
2. Did Roach's question ask anything concerning the circumstances surrounding the gas card? According to WACOPS, I could have been terminated for my answer. This is possibly the most egregious of WACOPS' claims and actions in this matter. Why? Because there is no way anyone could have ever been terminated under this scenario. Why? In order for someone to be terminated, they actually have had to have commit a crime, a serious violation of policy, or lie. None of which happened in this case. WACOPS' distortion of Roach's question is a serious breach of ethics on their part.

"Under current law, an arbitrator would consider the mitigating circumstances - that you were pre-approved for the practice and that you repaid the county - and that arbitrator would have had the option of reinstating your employment."

1. The fact here is that, "Under current law," this case would have never made it to an arbitrator because no chief or sheriff in their right mind would have terminated someone who had permission to use publicly-funded gas in their private vehicle. If they tried, their legal advisors would have stopped them because not only would such a termination result in arbitration, but it would also result in a lawsuit.
2. Note WACOPS' spin on the arbitrator's role. Remember that under the proposed Law Enforcement Integrity First bill, the arbitrator could not overturn the termination if they found that the sheriff or chief had acted properly. If the arbitrator found the sheriff or chief had acted improperly, they would be able to overturn the termination. This sentence is another example of WACOPS' untruthful portrayal of the issue in that the Law Enforcement Integrity First bill ensured the exact outcome stated here by WACOPS. In no way did the bill prevent an arbitrator from considering mitigating circumstances.

"This due process is what we are trying to protect."

1. Again, WACOPS attempted to paint the picture that the proposed legislation somehow destroyed due process. The fact is that every aspect of Due Process remained intact under the proposed legislation. The only thing that changed is after the arbitrator ensured that Due Process was followed, found that the chief or sheriff acted properly, and found that the violation actually occurred, the arbitrator was required to uphold the sheriff or chief's disciplinary decision.

Remember, WACOPS denied any knowledge that Senator Roach was going to ask the question. Kind of hard to believe that after reading this letter, isn't it? This letter would become a major problem for WACOPS.

Within two hours of WACOPS sending me this letter in an email, the DSA posted the letter on their website. This isn't the only place the letter would appear. Within a day of the letter being sent to me, I was contacted by people in Spokane County stating that they had also received the letter in the mail. They were not happy with WACOPS' accusations.

One of the people who had received the letter was a volunteer with the Spokane Police Department's community oriented policing effort (COPS). He stated that if I was guilty, then so was he, since he was also authorized to use his personal vehicle for his COPS duties and was given a gas card to fill his vehicle. It appeared that the letter had been sent both to COPS volunteers and volunteers of the Sheriff's Community Oriented Policing Effort (SCOPE) program volunteers.

It didn't stop there. Precinct committee officers of both the Democratic and Republican parties also received it. WACOPS would soon learn that regular folks did not share their opinion of the proposed legislation or of me.

I called the WACOPS Executive Director about the letter and asked her what was going on. She was very defensive and stated that WACOPS had been receiving returned copies of the letter for the past several days. She stated that WACOPS had not sent the letter. I told her that I had a hard time believing that since the letter was on WACOPS letterhead and was sent in a WACOPS envelope.

She stopped me there and told me to look closely at the envelope. She asked if I saw the WACOPS logo on the envelope. I stated that the envelope did not have the logo but did have the WACOPS address. She then told me to look at the post mark, reminding me that WACOPS was headquartered in Olympia. The letters had been mailed out of the Spokane area.

I then asked her, "So, you're telling me someone stole your identity?"

She was adamant that this was exactly what had happened. I told her that I would have the incident investigated by the postal service and FBI. Why the FBI? Public corruption is their area of responsibility. Since the stamps had a Liberty Bell on them, I suspected that someone from the Libertarian side of the Republican party was involved and that it was most likely an elected official.

I offered to help WACOPS clear their name since they were being hammered by the public over the letter. I told them that I would do a joint press release and conference with them to explain that someone had stolen their identity. My public information officer (PIO) and the WACOPS communications specialist began working on a joint message. WACOPS crafted and sent the following statement to my PIO on February 22, 2013:

The Washington Council of Police & Sheriffs (WACOPS), in the course of representing their membership in legislative deliberations, recently drafted and distributed two letters addressed to members of the Washington State Legislature and Sheriff Ozzie Knezovich. Electronic copies of these letters were also distributed to WACOPS membership and relevant stakeholders.

Several days after the first correspondence was released, WACOPS received returned mailings containing the letter addressed to legislators. The envelopes were printed as if to appear to be official association mailings to residents of the Spokane area, and included the label "Important Legislative Update." The return address provided on the envelopes was listed as the WACOPS office in Olympia. However, the post mark indicated that the letters were of local origin.

"I have been informed that the second letter, addressed to Sheriff Knezovich, has also been received by Spokane area residents," said [redacted], WACOPS Executive Director. "We are appreciative of the Sheriff's assistance in determining the source of these falsified mailings. While their content shows that we were at odds with Sheriff Knezovich in regard to a particular policy proposal, WACOPS stands united with him in disavowing such political tactics."

On the eve of sending out the joint press release, we were very curtly notified by WACOPS that they no longer wished to participate in a joint press release. They simply stated that while they admitted to writing the letter, they denied mailing it out. Of course, I asked what was up and was simply told there would be no joint press conference.

Interestingly, that same day, the Law Enforcement Integrity First legislation died in committee.

From February 15 to February 22, I had spent the majority of my time dealing with the fallout of the Senate hearing on multiple fronts. All the while, Senator Padden and I continued our attempt to work with WACOPS on acceptable language, only to see those efforts fail. There was also a media battle taking place at the local, state, and now a national level.

CBS This Morning did a story about our efforts to change state law. The program focused on how this was not just a Washington State issue, but a national issue. On March 6, 2013, the program aired a report: "How fired police officers often end up back on the job."

Police chiefs' mission is to serve and protect the public from criminals. But across the country, those chiefs are battling bad apples within their own departments.

The police chiefs are finding it nearly impossible to fire some of their own officers, in part because of arbitration and union rules.

When a police officer breaks the rules, or the law, he or she is disciplined, and in rare cases, fired. But often, that's not the end of the story. Officers appeal their cases to state arbitrators, civil service boards, or civilian commissions -- and many times end up back on the job.

In Oklahoma, a police lieutenant was fired for elbowing a handcuffed prisoner in the mouth.

In Omaha, Neb., several cops were fired after beating a man outside a hospital.

And in Philadelphia, a police lieutenant was fired after smacking a woman down at a disorderly street festival. He has appealed to an arbitrator and his chances of getting his job back are good. In Philadelphia, nine out of 10 cops fired by the police chief are reinstated by an outside arbitrator.

It's a problem across the country that is frustrating police chiefs and sheriffs.

Asked if he's fired people and had to have them come back, Los Angeles County Sheriff Lee Baca -- who runs the biggest sheriff's department in the U.S. -- said, "Yes, and I believe that that's the process."

CBS News senior correspondent John Miller, who served in ranking positions at both the New York and Los Angeles Police Departments, said, "I mean, you've got people out there that you've already come to a judgment shouldn't be out there. And somebody's superseded your judgment. How does that feel?"

Baca said, "Well, it-- it feels that you have no control over your resources to the extent you need to have. That our judgment becomes somewhat nonsignificant (sic) in these certain cases."

In an infamous Milwaukee case, an officer was fired after he was caught on a dashboard camera punching a handcuffed woman in the face. The city's Civilian Police Commission overruled the chief and reinstated the officer. Under pressure from an outraged community, a week later, the police commission re-fired the officer.

In Spokane Wash., the sheriff has fired deputies, only to see them back on the job. Sheriff Ozzie Knezovich said, "There's no clearly defined public policy against a law enforcement officer being dishonest."

So Knezovich went to the Washington State Legislature to change the law.

Knezovich said, "The only thing it changes in the law is that if an arbitrator finds that a deputy has committed these crimes, and/or they have been dishonest, the arbitrator can't overturn the sheriff's discipline at that point. As in, they can't say, 'Yes, you committed these crimes, but you're getting your job back.'"

CBS THIS MORNING

The police unions in Washington State oppose the law. They believe it gives one person too much power. [redacted], executive director of the Washington Council of Police and Sheriffs, said, "This legislation would allow a chief or a sheriff to make an accusation, investigate that accusation himself, be the judge and jury if that accusation was true, and then be the executor of the discipline for that."

But Knezovich believes he is the one person who is responsible for the officers under his command. Knezovich said, "I'm accountable to 471,000 people in Spokane County. They're the ones that will tell me when it's time to back down."

Knezovich testified for his bill in the Washington State Senate. It died quietly in committee without ever getting to the floor for a vote. But he'll try to bring it up again, and chiefs and sheriffs in other cities are watching.

As you can see, WACOPS had changed their line of attack by the time their Executive Director was interviewed for this program. I can tell you that she was none too happy to be sitting in front of a national camera. WACOPS' new message was that the legislation allowed sheriffs and chiefs to be judge, jury, and executioner when it came to disciplinary decisions. Again, WACOPS made false statements, but this time it was on the national stage.

On the day the CBS program aired, I received the following email from retired Chelan County Sheriff Mike Harum:

Ozzie,

If there is anything I can do to help get the legislature to expand on the previous bill making it a public policy that a law enforcement officer must be honest, please let me know. They were watered down greatly before they passed and need someone like you to change them.

I worked very hard on the previous bills in 2009/2010 and paid a great price in doing so. The unions came after me with a vengeance in 2010 and I lost re-election. They provided legal assistance and thousands of dollars to the current Sheriff of Chelan County. The union attorney represented two of the Deputies I terminated. He also represented [the defendant] in the Kitsap county decision.

I disciplined many deputies in my career as Sheriff and terminated three deputies for lying. Two of the terminated Deputies settled before arbitration and one just went to arbitration November 2012, the county is still waiting for that decision. I am not sure what the arbitrator will do but the chances of being returned to work is high.

Thank you for the work you are doing!

Mike Harum, Retired Chelan County Sheriff

If you remember, I was promised the same treatment that Sheriff Harum received by WACOPS during my meeting with them in Representative Parker's office. They were busy attempting to deliver on that promise. What WACOPS was beginning to realize though, or I suspect already knew, was that they had few allies. They learned from the letter incident that their allies were willing to throw them under a bus if necessary. WACOPS was not necessarily in control this time.

Those allies were also moving forward and had formed a Political Action Committee (PAC), which "surprisingly" had members of WACOPS on it.

Considering the above mailing. Those sorts of letter campaigns are expensive. Which means someone had to fund it. PACs have money. Until then, no one knew about this PAC. That was until they slipped up and played their hand prematurely. When one of the PAC's members was contacted by the media, they stated, "We don't want Ozzie to see us coming."

And you'll never guess what they named their PAC.

Chapter 8

Integrity First Political Action Committee

We don't want Ozzie to see us coming.

As the 2013 legislative session came to a close, the internal affairs investigator completed his investigation into my use of the gas card, and a nagging rumor that I was going to have an opponent in 2014 was getting louder. One of my former command staff, a jail captain I should have let go when I first became Sheriff, was telling people that he had found someone to run against me. That person was a City of Spokane police detective, Doug Orr.

Back in 2012, I noticed that Orr started showing up at many of my speaking engagements or public meetings. By December of that year, he had used the city's TV channel to tape a presentation before a Rotary Club. I could never understand how he had been given permission to use city assets in such a way, However, I'm glad he did so because the video gave me many talking points to use against him. Especially his take on domestic violence and how it was bad policy to arrest those who commit this crime.

I received a call from a good friend and retired jail lieutenant stating that he had just had lunch with that former jail captain. The jail captain told him that a PAC had been formed and they were supporting Orr to run against me. They were also meeting with the DSA concerning the upcoming election.

I then learned that the DSA had donated $2,500 to the PAC, now known as Integrity First, so they could investigate the crime statistics that had been released for 2012 and early 2013. Their goal was to create doubt in the public's mind that the crime stats were real. More bluntly, they were making the accusation that I had falsified my crime stats.

Before we go any further, it is important to understand the membership of the Integrity First PAC. The DSA claim was that the members had a long history of service with the Spokane County Sheriff's Office. That was their justification for support of the PAC's efforts.

The members were:

- My former friend, the retired Spokane County Sheriff's Office detective and past DSA president I mentioned earlier, who was also serving on the WACOPS executive board.
- A retired Spokane County Sheriff's Office lieutenant, who at one time was given the responsibility of running our internal affairs unit, only to be removed from that duty because of questions surrounding his veracity in the investigations he conducted. He retired shortly after the last investigation into his conduct. It may have had something to do with my telling him that if he came before me again for being untruthful, I would terminate him regardless of what my attorney advised me.
- A former member of my command staff, the jail captain mentioned above.

- My former Public Information Officer (PIO), a retired Spokane County Sheriff's Office sergeant. He had been PIO for the prior Sheriff. I had allowed him to remain in that capacity until the last six months of his employment with the Sheriff's Office, at which point he asked for a transfer, which he was granted. He then retired.

It is worth noting that the PIO and I had developed what I thought was a friendship, to the point that he said he was willing to serve as my PIO for my 2010 campaign. Seeing his name as part of this PAC was pretty much the ultimate betrayal.

If there was anyone within the Sheriff's Office, outside of the people who actually compiled our statistics, who should have debunked this claim, it would have been this man. He knew that there was only one way to really make me upset: give me bad stats or not correct those stats before I put them out. He saw me dress people down on more than one occasion because bad information had been put out to the public, and he didn't enjoy it either because he also knew that if we made this type of mistake, he would have to set up a press conference so we could correct the bad information.

So, these four retired Spokane County Sheriff's Office employees were the "official" founders of the PAC. Another retired Sheriff's Office employee would play a key role, a former undersheriff (a different undersheriff from the gas card accusations).

This group formed the base of the Integrity First PAC. As mentioned above, The DSA union supported the PAC's request because of the group's vast law enforcement experience. They'd say something like, "This group has over one hundred years of law enforcement experience." Of course, it is best to check and see the type and quality of that service.

About this time, I had a conversation with one of my contacts in the local media. I told her about the PAC and some of the claims my former PIO had been making. When she contacted him, he denied any knowledge of a PAC. He then said something that countered his claim of having no knowledge of the PAC, "We don't want Ozzie to see us coming."

His double speak to the media was really a bad move because the PAC had already registered with the Washington Public Disclosure Commission, and he was listed as one of the PAC's officers. This would not be the last public falsehood from the PAC. Their lies would grow more vile, and they targeted some very good people in an attempt to destroy my credibility with the citizens of Spokane County.

The Integrity First PAC wasted no time in launching a full-scale attack on me by stating that I had falsified the crime stats that had just been released. They had to make this claim for several reasons:

1. Their candidate, Doug Orr, had presented falsified crime stats during the recorded presentation to the Rotary Club, and I had been using those recordings to show Orr's crime stats for what they were: false.

2. In 2012, we had a major increase in property crimes, especially residential burglaries. By April 2012, residential burglary was off the charts. As a result, I formed a burglary task force, and the Sheriff's Office went to work arresting every burglar we could. The results can be summed up by a statement a burglar gave to one of our detectives when he was arrested and asked why he and his crew went to a neighboring county to commit a series of burglaries. "We know you are arresting everyone in Spokane County." And we were. By the end of 2012, we had seen an approximate fifty-two percent decrease in residential burglaries, and property crimes in general were also down significantly. The PAC could not allow such good work to stand.
3. As we covered in prior chapters, some candidates and campaigns in Spokane County purposely put out false information. The Integrity First PAC was following this political strategy. In doing so, it took me off message. Instead of talking about how property crimes were down, I was now defending our stats. The PAC was trying to tie their claims of false stats to the gas card incident in order to show that I had a very serious integrity issue. The sad part of this was that these men knew better. They had seen me deal with these types of issues and knew I had no tolerance for falsehoods. In order to discredit me, they knew they had to destroy my credibility concerning one of the things we had done best, lowering crime in Spokane County.

These attacks took a toll on some very good people. The integrity of the people who actually compiled the crime statistics was questioned, along with those who were directly responsible for the decrease in property crimes by arresting all those bad guys.

Doug Silver was in charge of our analytic unit. Doug is a great man and had been a captain in the Sheriff's Office before he retired and was rehired as a civilian employee to manage our crime data. I drove Doug crazy at times because I would ask him to double verify and even triple verify the stats I requested, depending on the importance of the project. It was Doug's reputation that was really under attack, and this bothered me greatly.

The fact is, the PAC knew my weakness. They knew that my people mean everything to me, and that I am highly protective of them. I could not believe the majority of this PAC would be part of such a malicious attack on the agency they claimed to value.

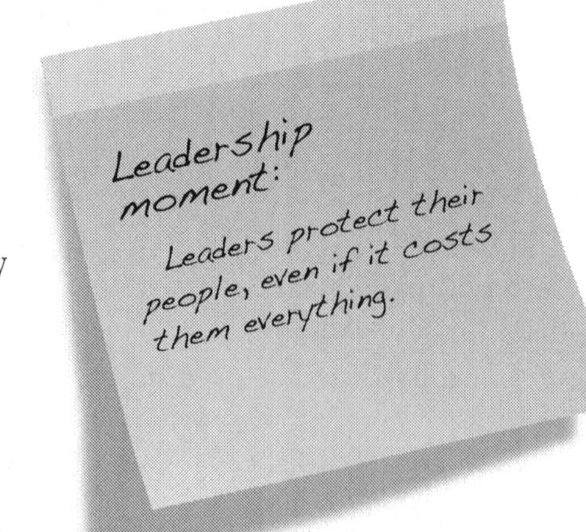

Leaders protect their people, even if it costs them everything.

Every leader needs to understand that their credibility is everything. It is something you guard and defend at all costs. But you must value your people more. Your people are everything. I owe everything to the men and women of the Sheriff's Office because they are the ones who are out there doing a great job, and it is their efforts that make me look good.

Leaders who do not understand that we do not accomplish things on our own are also the ones who do not understand the importance of the people who are actually doing the work. With that said, anytime someone attacks you, they are also attacking the people within your organization. When this happens, you have no choice but to defend them, and if necessary, be willing to take the shots being fired at them. Leaders protect their people at all costs.

When the PAC launched its full attack on me and the Sheriff's Office, the local media's reaction was not what the PAC had expected. On July 12, 2013, our local newspaper, The Spokesman Review, published a story that gave insight into the PAC's motives. The title was "Group claims sheriff too quick with discipline."

"We are really bothered by Ozzie's unrelenting focus on discipline and changing that law."

"We are all proud of the agency," [redacted] said, but the sheriff's focus has shifted to rooting out wrongdoing. He said Knezovich is too quick to mete out punishment, often disproportionate to the severity of the violation.

Some of the PAC's quotes in the article were:

Two days later, on July 14, 2013, the Spokesman Review ran the following Editorial:

Editorial: Integrity First ignores what the public needs

A new group challenging the leadership of Spokane County Sheriff Ozzie Knezovich has begun its campaign with a poor choice of name: Integrity First.

Irony First is more like it.

Can the four former department officials…truly believe their effort will get a sympathetic hearing from a public that has had it up to here with repeated incidents of abusive behavior and the lies used to try and cover it up?

In February, Spokane voters demanding responsible, respectful law enforcement gave the city's police ombudsman stronger authority to investigate citizen complaints against officers. The measure garnered almost 70 percent of the vote.

…The sheriff's effort to rid his department of the incompetent and incredible has been a slog since he took control in 2006. From a roster of 570 before the recent County Commission takeover of the jail, 47 resigned, retired or were terminated as a result of disciplinary action. Seven were deputies.

But he, like every other county sheriff in Washington, has tired of seeing dismissals or lesser sanctions overturned by arbitrators who do not necessarily question their findings of fact, but the punishment. One "self-admitted jailhouse clown" in Spokane got his job back despite putting a stripped, mentally ill inmate through a set of jumping jacks.

Real funny.

In the just-ended, endless legislative session, SB 5668, sponsored by Sens. Mike Padden and Michael Baumgartner, and HB 1225, with Rep. Kevin Parker among the sponsors, would have forbade arbitrators from overturning a dismissal if "clear and convincing evidence" shows the employee lied or committed an illegal act.

All 39 county sheriffs supported the measure, but the state's police chiefs were not yet on board. Knezovich says they are now, which will add new impetus to the legislative push.

Knezovich's foes, in their zeal to stop the bill, tried to slime him by implying he was willfully taking a free ride at taxpayers' expense by filling his gas tank on the county's dime. At the sheriff's request, city Police Ombudsman Tim Burns investigated. Burns' conclusion, released July 8:

The sheriff's use of a county credit card in May and June of 2006 – his first full months on the job – was the result of misinformation and stopped when the error was brought to his attention. He voluntarily reimbursed the county $372.30.

If he had taken the fuel stipend given his predecessor, it would have cost the county more than $1,100. Integrity First can try co-opting the principle, and misrepresenting its priorities, but their efforts should not shake the public's confidence in Knezovich. He and Straub are delivering much-needed reforms to law enforcement in the county and city.

They have their hands full.

The public's reaction was even harsher on the "Fab Four," as the members of the PAC were now being called by many within the Sheriff's Office. Again, it would be the outpouring of support from the public that made going through this easier. I've always been grateful for the support the people of Spokane County have given me.

And so it went for the rest of 2013. The Integrity First PAC filed numerous public records requests trying to find something to discredit me. In the end, they found nothing. However, due to a blunder on their part, I would learn they had been sending letters and emails to the Democratic and Republican parties, SCOPE volunteers, and COPS members.

On October 28, 2013, my former PIO sent an email blast to hundreds of Spokane County citizens. In the email, Integrity First claimed that they had not received the information they requested from the Sheriff's Office as a result of their Public Disclosure Requests. The trouble for him was that he forgot to blind cc the email list, so everyone could see who was on the list. This created a firestorm for Integrity First. The public pushback was quick and intense.

I received the following email from one of the recipients, a SCOPE member. It is a good representation of the sentiment from those on the list:

> I object to having ████ use email addresses acquired through the Sheriff's department in this manner. He is now a private citizen and has no right to the information. This is a violation of my right to privacy.

This blunder gave me the opportunity I could only have wished for, the ability to know who was receiving their letters and emails. More importantly, I now had the ability to finally respond.

I sent an email to the entire list, giving them a detailed account of the Sheriff's Office's efforts to fulfill the PAC's Public Disclosure Requests. Below is a portion of that response:

> …All of [the PAC's] requests have been fulfilled for weeks. [Their email] is very misleading, and a false statement as to the status of their requests…
>
> …What [they] did not tell you was that the material generated by their 1st of 4 public disclosure requests was over 2,000 pages long and the computer code had to be read line by line by an employee to ensure no names were improperly released. Once the PAC received the information, they immediately complained that the data was not what they had requested. It was exactly what they requested…
>
> Another falsehood [the] PAC has told the public is that they are not doing this out of politics and they have no candidate in mind to run for sheriff. Despite what they have told the public, this group is currently grooming a City of Spokane Police detective to run against me. I'm told he will announce next month.
>
> As those responsible for this PAC continue to send out emails, feel free to contact me and ask me questions.
>
> I have invited ████ to debate this issue at anytime. He has thus far refused.

Once again, Integrity First was caught lying to the public. Their requests had been filled for weeks, but they just didn't like the results. Integrity First was finding that there was no smoking gun to be found. Instead, they found that the Sheriff's Office had been telling the truth. Needless to say, they were not happy.

With the verification that Integrity First was behind the letters and emails, it finally made sense why WACOPS changed their mind on the joint press conference with me to clear their name. The Integrity First PAC was responsible for those letters that WACOPS had vehemently denied knowledge of. One of WACOPS' own members was on this PAC. Had WACOPS joined me in a press conference, they would have been seen as supporting me against the actions of one of their own members.

WACOPS, the DSA, and Integrity First must have realized, had the circumstances behind the letter become public knowledge, it would not have gone well for their efforts. Had the public been told that someone had stolen WACOPS' identity in order to attack my character, the ground swell of support for me would have overwhelmed them. WACOPS would have been faced with the dilemma of acknowledging that their own letter had been put out without their permission or knowledge by the PAC, tainting any future campaign against me and weakening the PAC's future bid to unseat me.

For months, I had invited the PAC's members to debate me on these issues, and they never did so. Instead, they spent their time presenting to groups affiliated with the Democratic Party. The interesting thing about this was that my opponent was running as a Republican. Well, sort of. He was actually a Democrat. The plan was to have him run as a Republican because Matt Shea had convinced Orr that Shea could split the Republican Party for Orr, resulting in the Democrats carrying the day for him. The Progressive Socialist wing of the Democratic Party was more than willing to join with Shea in this effort. The problem for them and Orr was, I have very strong support among working class Democrats, which make up the majority of the Democratic Party in Spokane County. Once again, I can only thank the people of Spokane County for their support. It has been an honor being your Sheriff.

How do I know that Orr was really a Democrat?

There was this problematic poll that an organization had conducted featuring Orr against me. Orr had contacted the organization trying to get them to drop their endorsement of me in favor of him. In his letter, he told them that he was running as a Democrat. You can see the poll for yourselves on the following page.

County Sheriff Knezovich Holds Commanding Lead

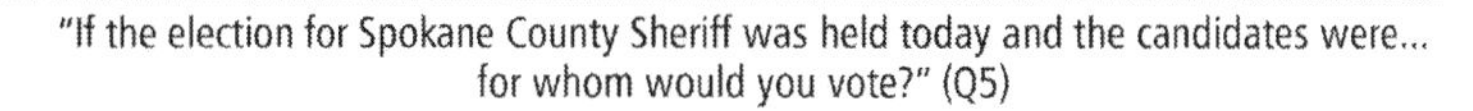

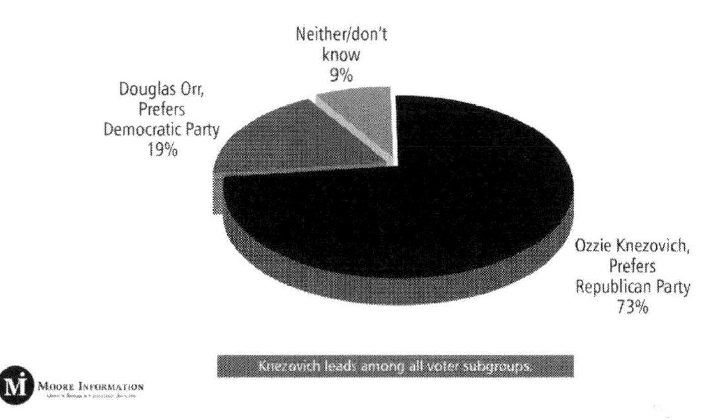

By summer's end in 2014, Integrity First would dissolve their PAC, stating they had accomplished their goals. If those goals were to verify that I and the Sheriff's Office were providing accurate information to the public, that we had reduced crime, and that we had reduced the number of lawsuits filed against the Sheriff's Office, then I guess they were successful. They were also successful in hurting their own candidate.

Despite dissolving, Integrity First still maintained their Facebook page and continued working with the DSA in support of their candidate, Doug Orr. Integrity First's actions in the 2014 Sheriff's election would pale compared to those of the DSA's. The DSA would actually attempt to use my religion against me.

Apparently, my standards are too high because of my religious beliefs.

Chapter 9

The Union Attacked Your Religion?

The Sheriff has a particular way he lives his life to a higher standard.

The DSA's attack was right in line with WACOPS warning that if I didn't back down, they were coming after me. I don't think anyone realized to what lengths they were willing to go.

Leadership moment:
Doing the right thing creates enemies.

Doing the right thing creates enemies.

As part of their strategy to make me pay for introducing the Integrity First Legislation, the DSA filed several unfair labor practices (ULPs) against me in reference to disciplinary issues. This was done to make me look like a heavy-handed totalitarian. Their ultimate goal was to run me out of office. Why?

For holding them accountable.

There are legitimate uses for ULPs when management steps outside established labor laws. However, unions often use UPLs in the same way they use votes of no confidence, which is to make management look bad. An unfair labor practice is any act committed by management that goes against established labor law. Unions file ULP complaints with the Public Employment Relations Commission (PERC). The PERC Commission has authority to hold hearings to determine if management has violated established labor laws and also hands down punitive measures if violations are found to have occurred. This isn't a one-edged sword. Management can also file a ULP against the union for violating these same labor laws.

Leadership moment:
Disciplinary issues are typically the hardest issues any leader faces.

Disciplinary issues are typically the hardest issues any leader faces.

Over the course of this book, I have attempted to portray why disciplinary issues are so challenging for leaders. These issues tend to drive a wedge between leaders and employees. This was the biggest point of division between Spokane County Sheriff leadership and line staff. Truth be told, it was also the biggest point of division between me and my command staff at one time.

One of my seventy-five terminations involved a deputy with a history of poor performance and even dangerous behavior. The most ironic aspect about this case was it had been the DSA's leadership who turned the deputy

in and demanded something be done. When I did, they fought me on the very discipline they had asked for, blaming me for being unfair. More specifically, it was the DSA vice president who demanded that an investigation be done. He asked the administration when we were going to "do something" about the performance of the deputy in question.

The issue involved a deputy who had a drinking problem and often didn't show up to work, which made it hard for some of his shift mates to get time off. It is worth noting that the DSA vice president was one of those shift mates. The deputy's job performance was poor and had been so for years. His issues with alcohol developed while working in an undercover capacity. I know that high stress professions can break people. This is particularly true in law enforcement.

When facing problems with staff, leaders need to remember that high stress professions can break people. This is particularly true in law enforcement.

The things an officer sees regularly are things I wish on no one. I firmly believe that we have a responsibility to see if we can salvage those who are broken.

This is the philosophy we took in trying to salvage the deputy's career. However, we rapidly found that there was no saving this deputy. His behavior, even after being placed on multiple performance improvement plans, spiraled out of control. At times, we found ourselves still investigating one complaint when the next one would come in. Within a three-month period, we had multiple performance issues under investigation concerning this deputy.

Leadership moment:
When facing problems with staff, leaders need to remember that high stress professions can break people. This is particularly true in law enforcement.

The day before he was terminated, I spoke with the DSA president. I told him that I saw no other alternative and that we had tried everything we could to turn the deputy around. He left me with the impression that he understood and agreed. At no time during the multiple discussions concerning the deputy did the DSA state they had issues with the termination. Quite the opposite, the DSA stated they could understand the administration's frustration and position on the matter. The VP actually complained that the investigator had failed to finish one of the investigations against the deputy AFTER the deputy had been terminated. The investigation was not finished because the deputy had already been terminated.

You can understand my surprise when the DSA went on to fight me for terminating the deputy. I was told that they did want him held accountable but not that accountable. Remember this attitude?

My head really hurt upon hearing that logic. This group demanded something be done, complained that we were not doing it fast enough, and then fought the outcome everyone knew was coming. And this is not the craziest part of this story. The DSA itself then abandoned the deputy and dropped his demand to go to arbitration. Why? Because the deputy came to a meeting with the DSA's attorney sloppy drunk.

Go figure.

Unfair Labor Practice Accusations

Some people have asked me, "Sheriff, how do you have such a memory of what happened in all these cases?"

Well, that would be because I wrote the details of the incident down, way back in 2007.

Leadership moment:

Any time you deal with a high priority issue, take notes.

Any time you deal with a high priority issue, take notes.

Whenever I have a meeting or have any dealings with issues that I judge to be a high priority, I take notes or commit the details of the meeting to writing shortly thereafter.

The VP I mentioned would become the president of the DSA. Under his leadership, the DSA would see its darkest period, a period in which it would lose the public's trust and the credibility it had enjoyed with the public for years. The results of his actions would lead the DSA to file three failed unfair labor practice (ULP) complaints on me during two elections and would also result in the county filing and winning an ULP on the DSA for regressive bargaining.

The problem with the DSA started with discipline, but it spread to other areas. The DSA leadership took a "fight Ozzie on everything at all costs" attitude on every issue. The sad thing is that they hurt their own membership. They fought my administration when we were trying to save the jobs, ranks, and benefits of the deputies.

One such issue was our attempt to save four corporal positions and maintain patrol staffing levels. After months of negotiating with the DSA on the issue, we thought we had an agreement. The president sent us an email on behalf of the DSA executive board which read in part, "The SCDSA does not have any problems with the idea of allowing the 4 corporals who were slated for demotion remaining corporals but being assigned to patrol…"

We agreed to their conditions in order to save the four positions, only to have the DSA backtrack and file a ULP on us for doing exactly what they had asked us to.

For those leaders residing in a union rights state, one thing to remember is that unions use grievances and ULPs much like votes of no confidence.

Unions file grievances and ULPs to show that your administration is corrupt, inept, and heavy handed, or that you are violating labor laws. As a result, they try to gain public sympathy and either force you to agree to their terms on an issue or force you out of your job or office.

This is why you should do your best to know labor laws, have a good relationship with the public, and keep notes of all your dealings with the unions. This was a hard-learned lesson for me. I come from a background where a man's word is his bond and a handshake is all that was needed. Not so much anymore. I cannot repeat this enough. Keep good notes and get everything in writing.

The DSA filed their first ULP on me in 2010, an election year. They were trying to flex their muscles and show me that if I did not fall into line, they would get rid of me. It didn't work, and their ULP was ruled to be unfounded.

As the next election approached in 2014, they turned their support to Doug Orr, a City of Spokane Police detective. The DSA president at the time pulled out all the stops, including attacking his own DSA members. This was possibly the most despicable part of the union's actions in their attempt to unseat me. This is when I learned that those who support leaders will often become targets themselves.

During that election, the DSA, along with WACOPS, the Integrity First PAC (before they dissolved), and their supporters attacked some very good and honorable people in their zeal to get rid of me. For me, this was the hardest part of that election: the fact that anyone who supported me was now a target. I had a hard time watching this happen. I found myself saying one too many times, "I'm your target. Go ahead and come after me, but leave my deputies and friends out of it." Little did I know that my family and my religion would be next.

The challenge in writing this book was not to get lost in all of the "dirty deeds" that happened while the unions worked to follow through with their threat to come after me. I've limited the rest of the book to four events that stand out the most when going through the volumes of material I have collected. They came after my best staff, my reputation, my religion, and finally, the safety of my family.

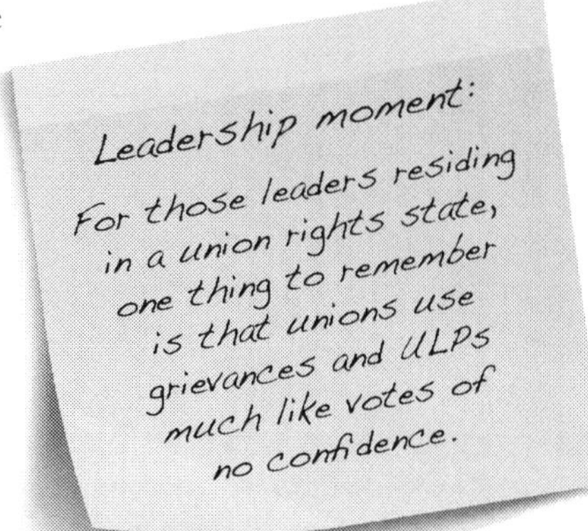

Event 1: The Brady Accusation

Around the first of July 2014, just a few weeks before the ballots for the primary election would be sent out, I received a panicked call to tune into the KXLY Radio's The Rick Rydell Show on AM 920. A caller had just announced the DSA would be making a formal announcement that day concerning the fact that the sergeant in charge of our internal affairs (IA) unit was a Brady officer.

Remember, being labeled a Brady officer is basically the kiss of death for a law enforcement officer because it implies that you have a sustained finding of being a liar. You can only imagine what it means for an agency to have the head of its IA office be labeled as such. It would put into question every IA investigation the sergeant was in charge of.

I was stunned. Not because of the possible ramifications for me, but because I could not believe that the DSA would stoop to such a new low. Especially because the person they were slandering was one of their own members, and more importantly because this sergeant is possibly the most honorable man I have ever had the pleasure of working with.

I immediately called one of the only DSA leaders I had any respect left for and asked what the hell the DSA was doing. He immediately stated, "Sheriff, I warned them not to do this. I told them this was a bad move."

I told him that three things would most likely result from this:

1. an investigation into the claim;
2. an investigation into the DSA if the claim was found to be false; and
3. if he was smart, a lawsuit filed by the IA sergeant against the DSA for defamation.

The ironic thing was that the caller prematurely made his "Breaking News" flash on The Rick Rydell Show, rather than waiting for the formal announcement to be made. The caller was a retired California detective living in Spokane who had been a thorn in the agency's side for years. The DSA immediately went into crisis management mode and denied any involvement in the matter.

The resulting investigation into the claim found that at no time was the sergeant in question found to have lied. We also found that the former undersheriff who was working with the Integrity First PAC was involved in the matter. He had acted as a private investigator for the DSA in trying to dig up dirt on the sergeant. Well, it goes without saying that the former undersheriff did have first-hand experience with

our IA sergeant because the sergeant and I had caught him and the California detective in false statements in the past.

Next came an investigation into the DSA president. As stated above, when that caller prematurely let the cat out of the bag, the DSA went into crisis management. The DSA president called Undersheriff Mark Werner, the Spokane Valley Police Chief. He told Chief Werner the DSA had received information that my IA investigator had resigned in lieu of termination amongst allegations of untruthfulness, thereby potentially making him a "Brady Officer." He stated that the DSA was not going to do anything with the information other than report it to Undersheriff Werner.

During the investigation, the DSA president would provide Undersheriff Werner with those documents, which he had "anonymously" received in the mail at his personal residence. He handed over everything but the envelope he had received them in. When Undersheriff Werner told me this, I said, "Everything but the envelope?"

During the IA investigation into the allegations leveled at our IA sergeant, we asked the former undersheriff if he had sent the information to the DSA. He stated that he would have to see the writing on the envelope to determine if he had sent it. And now the DSA president claimed that he no longer had the envelope. You may be thinking, "Well, that was convenient. Now there's no chance of comparing the handwriting on the envelope." You are right. Even more interesting, before he would turn the documents over, he requested that Undersheriff Werner order him to do so. Nice CYA, cover your backside, move on the DSA president's part. Undersheriff Werner did so and received the documents.

The IA sergeant followed with a complaint filed on the DSA president for disparaging a fellow member of the agency. During that investigation, it was learned that the president was only following our agency's policy. He claimed that once he had information, he had the responsibility to immediately report it. The problem the DSA president was facing was that he ignored the "immediately." It appears that he sat on the information and shared it with the retired California detective. This brought questions about the timing of when the DSA planned to present the information to the administration. It seems that they sat on this information until just before the primary ballots were to be mailed out to Spokane County voters. The other problem for the DSA president was if he had a duty to turn the information in, then why did he request that Undersheriff Werner order him to turn them in?

If reading this makes you shake your head, you now know what I felt like when dealing with this.

The retired California detective hounded the Sheriff's Office PIO for information concerning the IA investigation on nearly a daily basis. He did his best to try to stir the story in the media, social media, and again on the The Rick Rydell Show in an attempt to influence the primary election with this information. In an email sent on July 8, 2014 to my PIO, the California detective stated, "I not (sic) discuss this publicly until I knew the DSA provided this info to the Department." A clear indication that he was in contact with members of the DSA prior to publicly spreading this unfounded rumor.

The sad thing about this incident is that those who perpetrated it got off. My legal advisor suggested that the complaint be dropped because the union president was protected due to his status.

You may be wondering why there was no lawsuit to clear the IA sergeant's name?

Well, that's not as easy to do as people think. It is very difficult for a law enforcement officer to sue someone because we are considered public figures. Attorneys do not take these cases on contingency, like they do when people sue us. A lawsuit to reclaim your name will cost $20,000 – $40,000. In the end, the good guys get their reputations smeared and those who commit this type of defamation simply sit back and laugh at the damage. In the end, even though the investigation found none of the allegations against the sergeant were true, he still had to endure the sting of having the allegation made in such a public manner.

Event 2: The Affair

Right after this event, I received a phone call from a supporter telling me that someone was back on the The Rick Rydell Show stating that I was having an affair with the woman who makes my campaign signs. She said, "Man, your race is getting dirty."

Yes folks, not only did they try to make me out to be a liar and a thief, but I was also called a womanizer. When I told my sign lady about the claim, she was furious. My wife was not all that happy either.

I'll give you three guesses as to who was behind this rumor. You got it. The former undersheriff and his friend, the retired detective from California. A third man was now in the picture, a man I'll just call Cecil. He is the type of individual who deserves no identification or press, so I will not offer anything beyond that pseudonym.

You may be asking how I know that these individuals were behind this new rumor. Because the retired California detective put it in an email to the Spokane Police Department. On October 30, 2014, the email states, "…There is information that Knezovich has a 'girlfriend.' What the actual relationship [is] between the two is unknown. They spend a lot of time together…She owns a political sign company."

The claim that we spent a lot of time together is interesting. I think I met with my sign person about five times during that campaign. Once at the beginning to lineout sign orders and strategy, once to meet with a political figure from the Valley, once to get pictures with that same political figure when she endorsed me, and twice to pick up signs.

Why did they start this rumor? Well, my sign person was able to get me the above-mentioned endorsement. The former undersheriff had worked very hard to persuade the political figure in question to endorse Orr, and they nearly did. That was until I met with the political figure myself and gave her documentation that showed that Orr and his team were not being truthful with her. Remember what I said about keeping notes and documents? They come in handy when you have to defend yourself and your agency against these types of unethical attacks. I would learn that the former undersheriff was furious when I received her endorsement instead of Orr.

Event 3: My Religion

The next attack launched by the DSA was the ULP complaint they filed against me for terminating a deputy for having sex on duty. This was an amazing ULP to read. In it, I learned that my standards were too high due to my religion, and that I was forcing my religious standards on the secular position of my deputies.

I learned that the ULP had gone public when a reporter stated that the DSA president had contacted the local paper. I think the reporter may have spilled a little more than he should have by telling me this.

Apparently, the DSA president didn't realize that the newspaper has ways of tracking emails back to those who sent them. I learned from the reporter that the sender used a fake name and email account when he sent the email and that the paper had tracked it. When I pressed the reporter for how he knew about the ULP's contents, and how he knew who had sent it to the newspaper, he told me that it came from an account registered to the DSA president. Well, the press had a field day with its contents.

This was an article written by Doug Clark of the The Spokesman Review. Here it is in its entirety:

Doug Clark: Union attack on Ozzie Knezovich's faith bigoted, sleazy

Sure, I knew the deputy sheriffs' union had it in for Spokane County Sheriff Ozzie Knezovich.

The sheriff believes anyone worthy of wearing a badge should be able to hold off from doing the dance with no pants until after the shift ends.

While the union's attitude is more like …

"Don't come a-knockin' if the squad car's a-rockin'."

Differences this vast are bound to cause, um, friction.

Sarcasm aside, never in my wildest imaginings did I think these union reptiles would crawl so low as to try to use the sheriff's choice of churches against him.

But read it and weep, my friends.

The ugly truth is found on page 3 of an unfair labor practice complaint that the Spokane County Deputy Sheriffs Association filed recently against Knezovich.

The action comes in response to the sheriff's firing of [redacted] last summer for having sex on duty.

And I quote…

"Knezovich is an adherent to the Mormon religion.

"As established in his disciplinary decisions, Knezovich has reflected a belief that personal morality consistent with the tenets of the Mormon faith should be used as a guide to determine whether or not an appointed Spokane deputy sheriff should be subject to discipline."

Keep going. It gets better.

"The Association, on the other hand, believes that both the sheriff and deputy sheriff position are secular offices and should be guided by secular legal norms alone and …"

Ohhh, I get it.

The sheriff didn't fire [redacted] because of some generally accepted morality that on-duty cops should have the self-restraint to keep their zippers zipped. That was just Ozzie's Mormonism talking.

Are you as offended by this as I am? I hope so.

Where the sheriff chooses to worship should be nobody's business. Using it as a political talking point in a labor dispute is about as sleazy and shameful as it gets.

"It's 2014. These types of biases are supposed to be gone," the sheriff said during an interview this week about the complaint.

Knezovich told me he is adamant to never mix his faith with his lawman duties.

"I don't mention religion," he added, "I won't."

If you want to blame anyone for the sheriff's hair-trigger sense of right and wrong, blame George Washington and Abraham Lincoln.

Those are the role models Knezovich said he most admired as a kid.

The union's taking a shot at his denomination, he said, is "taking a shot at all Christian denominations."

He's right. Although you can bet that the deputy association would never have gone down this road were Knezovich Catholic or Baptist.

Mormonism is just different enough for gutless bigots to pick on.

What the deputy sheriff association doesn't know, however, is how badly this will bite them in the backside.

With apologies to old George and Honest Abe, the values Knezovich represents the most are those held by the folks who vote and pay taxes and don't care for bad cops.

Since his appointment as sheriff in 2006, Knezovich has never been shy about voicing his belief that law enforcers should be held to the highest standards, collective bargaining contracts be damned.

Knezovich has twice pushed for legislation to make it easier to terminate or decertify cops who break the law or lie like rugs while on duty.

All that said, it's important to note that Knezovich didn't fire…outright.

He gave the deputy a second chance to save his job by signing a "last-chance agreement." That would have allowed [redacted] to be terminated and then reinstated after a 90-day suspension with limited rights to file future grievances.

It was more of a break than I would have given this clown.

Not that it matters. The deputy association didn't like the terms and…dumbly refused to sign.

Bet that deal doesn't look so bad right now, huh?

Before you ask, yes, I was going to give the deputy a last chance agreement. Why? The deputy had been a very good employee and had been involved in setting up many charitable community relation events. He also appeared to have been honest about the incident. I did say "appeared." I would come to find that maybe he wasn't so honest about what had happened concerning this event. This was my mistake I believed him and didn't verify what he told me.

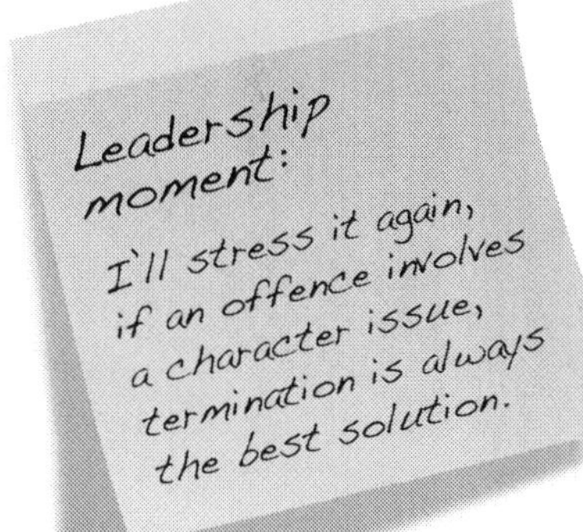

If the disciplinary issue involves a character issue the best course of action is termination.

Harsh? Not really, and here's why. I know of no class or school I can send a grown person to where they will learn how to tell the truth. The fact is, there are things you can't fix, and character is one of them. Every instance in which I have given someone a second chance after a breach of character has come back to haunt me and the agency in some way.

Character matters, folks. I ask you, if you knew someone had a history of lying, would you hire them? If the answer is no, then why would you keep them?

For me, I haven't had the luxury of holding firm to this standard because, as you know by now, the Washington State Supreme Court has made it nearly impossible to do so. As a result of our Supreme Court's actions, my philosophy is simple: Take me to arbitration. If you get your job back, then that's on the arbitrator. I've done my job.

At the end of the day, I did terminate the deputy because the union refused to sign the last chance agreement, which stated that the deputy would be terminated and that he would be reinstated under the terms and conditions of the agreement. The DSA did not like the word "termination." I was not willing to give the deputy the last chance without the termination language. Why? Because that is what should happen if an officer has sex on duty. They should be terminated. So, he was terminated.

The DSA filed for arbitration to get the deputy's job back, along with the now infamous ULP.

The deputies of the Spokane County Sheriff's Office were very angry about the DSA's handling of this matter and the wording of this ULP. The title of this chapter is actually a quote from a post made in an attempt to explain these actions to their membership. This is how the VP tried to explain this attack on my religion:

> *"...The religious aspect was placed in there by Jim Cline, the attorney representing the DSA in this matter. What Jim was trying to do is paint a picture that the Sheriff has a particular way he lives his life to a higher standard. That standard is not how some in this department live their lives..."*

There is a problem with this explanation. The DSA president originally blamed the VP for how the ULP was written. When their membership went after them, it was suddenly their attorney's fault.

Every time I read this, all I can think is, "What higher standards do I live by?" I don't care if religious or secular standards are being used to evaluate this incident, sex on duty is wrong.

The VP asked if I would let the deputy resign in lieu of termination, and I agreed to do so. Shortly after this, the deputy contacted me and asked for a meeting, a meeting in which I violated one of my own leadership rules: I met with the deputy alone. Why? I thought I knew him, and he had always been a solid person. I would pay a price for this decision.

Never meet with someone who is under investigation alone.

Even if you know and think you can trust them. It will never go well. Always have someone with you and either take notes or have the meeting recorded. Fail to do this at your own risk.

During the meeting, I told the deputy that his actions were terminal. I told him that I had run the incident by some of my peers and that only one of them said I should give him a second chance. I lamented that it may not seem right that a whole career could come down to ninety seconds of bad decision making; however, that is what happens. I have seen ninety seconds of bad decision making cost many people a career.

I explained to him the only way I would consider allowing him to remain employed was if he agreed to a last chance agreement in which he would be terminated and then brought back under very strict guidelines. He would receive a sixty-day suspension and lose any of his specialty assignments. I said if he didn't think he could agree to these terms, there was nothing more I was willing to do. The deputy was very emotional during the meeting and very appreciative of the chance to keep his career. He stated that he was willing to accept the terms of the agreement.

Well, that is until the DSA refused to sign the agreement.

The DSA's depiction of my meeting with the deputy in the body of their ULP was one of the—okay, I can't even find the proper word for it—worst examples of untruth I have seen.

Well, maybe not. Being accused of assault was actually the most—again, I can't find the proper word—appalling example of untruth I have ever lived through.

Accused of an assault?

Yes.

If you are wondering how that turned out, well, the same as every one of their accusations. After being dragged through the mud again, no assault was found.

You may be asking yourself, does this type of character assassination ever stop? No, it didn't stop after that election, nor has it stopped in my last term. And I suppose it never will. It is truly something that is just part of the leadership experience.

Does it get easier to live with? Ask yourself this question, "Do you think you could ever get used to being called a liar, a thief, a bully, etc.? No, it doesn't get easier. However, you do learn how to live with it.

Leadership moment:
Never meet with someone who is under investigation alone.

When you hold to your agency's values, those who did not get their way or who have paid the price for dishonoring their badge become angry to the point of vindictiveness. Staying true to who you are and the values you hold will help you get through the bad times.

You have to constantly remember who you are, and remind yourself of what you believe in, what you hold to be true, and what your values are. It is too easy to devolve and to begin acting like your detractors. This is something you never want to do. Their actions make it way too easy to slide down the path of hate, revenge, and such conduct.

If you believe in the concept of honor, you can't act like those who do such things. The true struggle is not to become as they are. We must hold on to the values we have chosen to live by. At times, that is a daily struggle, folks.

Leadership moment:

At times, when you hold to your agency's values, those who did not get their way or who have paid the price for dishonoring their badge become angry to the point of vindictiveness. They will attempt to destroy your reputation, and their words will hurt. It will cut you to your soul. Staying true to who you are and the values you hold will help you get through the bad times.

Chapter 10
My Last Ride

I won the 2014 election with seventy-one percent of the popular vote. At the end of our 2014 campaign, my wife looked at me and said, "Please don't run again."

Her words, at times, still echo in my heart. My wife maintained her request that I not run again until December 2017. By this time, we had lived under a death threat for over a year.

The FBI investigated these threats. The FBI and I were both amazed to learn that you can threaten to kill a sheriff and get away with it. The prosecutors at both the county and federal level refused to pursue charges. Politics.

I've chosen not to give the person responsible for that threat any more energy, so I will end that story here.

On December 28, 2017, as we were driving home after spending Christmas with our kids, my wife looked at me and said, "I know you love your agency and our community and that you still have some things you would like to accomplish for them. I'm okay with one last run. But this is the last run."

At the beginning of my 2018 re-election campaign, I made it clear that this would be my last ride as Sheriff of Spokane County.

My 2018 election was the strangest, and sadly most politically sick, election of my career as an elected official. We won by eighty-six percent of the popular vote. In 2022, I will close this chapter of my life. It's nice to be ending this journey on my terms. Something I thank the man upstairs for often.

As I move into my fourth, and last, term as the elected Sheriff of Spokane County, I find myself reflecting on the events of the past fourteen years. Events that remind me of the saying, "Heavy is the head that wears the crown."

I find myself hoping that I've passed the passion I have for what I do to the next generation of deputies and their leaders soon to take my place. Have I instilled in them the concept of living by our values to the point that it is now part of our agency's culture? Do our actions reflect our values? Do our actions reflect who we claim to be?

My hope is that this book has shown the importance of upholding one's personal honor and the honor of the law enforcement profession as a whole. It is, in some respects, my testament of the price that comes with doing the right thing. It is a price that you, your family, your friends, and those close to you will pay, should you decide honor is worth fighting for.

Perhaps my hope was realized in an email from one of my deputies:

> Sheriff Knezovich,
>
> I appreciate the time you've allowed me to contemplate accepting the Sheriff's Star Award. I am humbled and grateful to be considered… I would be honored to accept this award.
>
> It can be difficult for me to accept recognition for integrity-based behavior because as you know, doing the right thing should be what every law enforcement professional is all about; however, I acknowledge that these opportunities can be few and far between. Thank you very much for recognizing me.

This young deputy came forward concerning misconduct on the part of one of our supervisors. She didn't have to because she was an uninvolved party. It pains me to say that other supervisors in our agency viciously attacked her credibility and character. Honor has a price. She paid it.

As I stated in the prologue, my profession is under attack. The drumbeat is that police officers get away with everything and are never held accountable. This is a false narrative, largely driven by activists and media bias.

Law enforcement leaders do attempt to hold our own accountable. There are many great law enforcement leaders who have done their best to hold our profession accountable such as: former Philadelphia Police Commissioner Charles Ramey, Pierce County Washington Sheriff Paul Pastor, Chief Anne Kirkpatrick, Sheriff Mike Harum, and scores of other sheriffs and chiefs I have met in my career. They all laid everything on the line to ensure our profession lived up to its true calling.

That calling?

To protect and defend the rights of We the People. Rights which were listed in the Constitution of the United States of America by James Madison as a reminder of the God-given rights held by the People before the Constitution was ever established. Thomas Jefferson listed some of these rights in the Declaration of Independence:

> *We hold these truths to be self-evident, that all men are created equal, that they are endowed by their Creator with certain unalienable Rights, that among these are Life, Liberty and the pursuit of Happiness.—That to secure these rights, Governments are instituted among Men, deriving their just powers from the consent of the governed…*

I know one day, when We the People are done tearing our nation apart, we as a united nation will find a way to truly live up to these words. And then all will be treated as equal and all will have a chance to live Life, with

Liberty and justice for all. Americans everywhere will be able to pursue Happiness for themselves, their families, and their fellow countrymen. Free from fear and those who would do them harm.

The sad reality of our current political environment is that politicians, activists, and some of the media cry for accountability, and then they are the first to turn a deaf ear when their law enforcement leaders come to them and ask for help to rid our profession of the few bad apples.

In contrast, when a high-profile shooting happens, these same politicians, activists, and media demand passage or support of new laws designed to find ways to put law enforcement officers in jail for doing the job they and the public sent them out to do. They do this by hiding behind a myth that law enforcement officers haven't been given proper training or that they need more training. The uncomfortable truth is that most law enforcement officers in this country are highly trained professionals.

Training is not what's truly needed. What's needed is for these same politicians, activists, and media to recognize how they are hurting our profession. Yes, sometimes one bad actor is allowed to get away with misdeeds. That is true. But it is also true that, as a profession, we have very few bad apples. The true failure happens when that bad apple is removed from our profession and is then given their job back. Given their job back by a system that has forgotten one imperative, we took an Oath to live by a higher set of values.

The majority of law enforcement leaders want to hold our profession to high standards and to ensure we live by the high values we claim to have. But we need help to ensure that those unfit to wear the badge permanently lose the privilege of wearing it.

The next time you hear of a sheriff or a chief who is trying to change a state law in hopes of holding bad officers accountable, help them. Help us keep law enforcement the values-based profession it truly is. Pressure your politicians to do the right thing!

To all law enforcement leaders, it's time to choose if you really believe that duty, honor, and community still mean something. Do we really believe in our Code of Honor, or is it just letters that hang on a wall? You must ensure that you set high standards for yourself and those around you. In doing so, you preserve the most precious thing we have. The thing which enables you to protect your community and make it a safe place to live, work, and raise your family. What is that precious thing?

The public's trust.

It is time for leaders to breathe life back into the art of leadership. We need leaders willing to take a stand. If we say that we live by a certain set of values, then we must actually live by them.

Honor has a price. It's time to decide if we are willing to pay it.

Sources

"Editorial: Integrity First Ignores What the Public Needs."
The Spokesman-Review, July 14, 2013.
https://www.spokesman.com/stories/2013/jul/14/editorial-integrity-first-ignores-what-the-public

"Editorial: Sheriff, Chief Need Power to Restore Public Trust."
The Spokesman-Review, January 11, 2012.
https://www.spokesman.com/stories/2012/jan/11/editorial-sheriff-chief-need-power-to-restore

"How Fired Police Officers Often End up Back on the Job."
CBS This Morning, March 6, 2013.

Clark, Doug. "Doug Clark: Union Attack on Ozzie Knezovich's Faith Bigoted, Sleazy."
The Spokesman-Review, February 16, 2014.
http://www.spokesman.com/stories/2014/feb/16/doug-clark-union-attack-on-ozzie-knezovichs-faith

Gilmartin, Kevin M. Emotional Survival for Law Enforcement: A Guide for Officers & Their Families.
Tucson, AZ: E-S Press, 2002.

KITSAP COUNTY DEPUTY SHERIFF GUILD v. KITSAP COUNTY, 34321-5-II
KITSAP COUNTY DEPUTY SHERIFF GUILD v. KITSAP COUNTY §
(June 26, 2007).
caselaw.findlaw.com/wa-court-of-appeals/1177610.html

Kline, Delvin, Brandland, and Hargrove. Requiring law enforcement officers to be honest and truthful., SB Requiring law enforcement officers to be honest and truthful. § (n.d.).
https://app.leg.wa.gov/billsummary?BillNumber=6590&Year=2009

Prager, Mike. "Group Claims Sheriff Too Quick with Discipline."
The Spokesman-Review, July 12, 2013.
https://www.google.com/search?client=safari&rls=en&q=group-claims- sheriff-too-quick-with-discipline&ie=UTF-8&oe=UTF-8

Rick Rydell Radio Show. Spokane, WA:
KXLY, 2014.

RICKERT v. STATE PUBLIC DISCLOSURE COMMISSION, 77769-1
RICKERT v. STATE PUBLIC DISCLOSURE COMMISSION §
(Oct. 4, 2007).
http:// caselaw.findlaw.com/wa-supreme-court/1379647.html

Tartaro, Christine. "Section 1983 Liability And Custodial Suicide."
Californian Journal of Health Promotion 3, no. 2 (January 2005): 113–24.
https://doi.org/10.32398/cjhp.v3i2.1768